COMMUNITY POWER
AND
POLITICAL THEORY

BY NELSON W. POLSBY

New Haven and London, Yale University Press

Distributed in Great Britain, Europe, Asia,
and Africa by Yale University Press Ltd.,
London; in Canada by McGill-Queen's University
Press, Montreal; and in Mexico by
Centro Interamericano de Libros
Académicos, Mexico City.

Library of Congress catalog card number:
63–7946

Originally published as Volume 7 in the
Yale Studies in Political Science, edited
by David Horne, and under the
direction of the Department of
Political Science.

For E.W.P. and in memory of D.P. II

Preface

This book grew out of a study of New Haven, Connecticut, but it is not primarily about New Haven at all. In 1957 I was asked by Robert Dahl to join him and Raymond Wolfinger in an exploration of leadership and decision-making in New Haven. Wolfinger, my fellow graduate student, was to go into City Hall for a year's internship with New Haven's Development Administrator and with the Mayor. His job was to keep his eyes open and report what he found. My duties were less clear. A year of prior training as a graduate student in sociology had given me a nodding acquaintance with scholarly literature on the topic we were taking up in New Haven. Slowly I began to reread more carefully the leading community studies, looking for leads and hypotheses which would help us in studying New Haven. Dahl and Wolfinger did the same, and, in the course of a conversation which extended fitfully over perhaps four months, all of us reached the conclusion that previous studies of "community power," as they were usually styled, would not help us as much as we had hoped and expected.

I undertook to discover in detail why this was so, and the book which follows is the result. I attempt here to set the New Haven study into the context provided by previous work, showing explicitly where and how and to a certain extent why the New Haven study diverges from what seems to be the mainstream of community power studies. Hence this book is not principally about New Haven, although it depends in at least three ways on information gathered about New Haven.

First, the demands of doing research in an actual field situation (in which I took part) originally raised the theoretical problems dealt with here. The difficulties of theory which I discuss are not, I think, mere matters of taste but rather have consequences in the real world of research.

Secondly, the "payoffs" of the alternative research design adumbrated and defended in this volume are made explicitly manifest in the companion volumes reporting the results of the New Haven research: Robert Dahl's *Who Governs? Democracy and Power in an American City* (New Haven, 1961) and Raymond E. Wolfinger's forthcoming *The Politics of*

Progress. These works describe in detail the operations of the political order of New Haven. I think they lend to my argument for a pluralistic theory a persuasiveness far greater than the words in this book alone could convey.

Finally, I rely heavily on data developed in New Haven to test the theory I found in the literature. Since a major finding of this book is that this theory had not been tested adequately, the New Haven research made possible an attempt to improve on previous efforts at verification.

As befits a reincarnated doctoral dissertation, originally presented to The Department of Political Science at Yale University, this study is addressed primarily to the community of scholars; only they are likely to be familiar with the literature treated here. Some people may feel that my reading of this literature is idiosyncratic, not to say perverse. I have taken the rather tedious but necessary precaution of quoting at length from each of the works I have reinterpreted in order to forestall, if possible, raising the suspicion that instead of having read these works in a new way I have not read them at all. My purpose throughout has been to ascertain the state of "scientific" knowledge about power and policy-making in local communities. I hope the reappraisal I have made will help in future research on this topic, and I trust the pages that follow will be read with this goal in mind.

Nelson W. Polsby

Middletown, Connecticut
August 3, 1962

Acknowledgments

I owe an especially great debt to Robert A. Dahl. His administrative and personal generosity, creativity, and capacity for bringing order out of chaos are, I fear, only wanly reflected in these pages. Raymond E. Wolfinger gave much to this study as well. His contribution was not confined to the information about New Haven politics which he painstakingly gathered at great risk to life, limb, and sanity, and shared with me, but also included many discussions in which he helped greatly to clarify my thoughts.

Others kept me amply supplied with a running fire of criticism, comment, suggestion, and encouragement. This was especially true of an extraordinarily stimulating group of friends and teachers at Yale, including Charles E. Lindblom, Aaron B. Wildavsky, Fred I. Greenstein, Theodore J. Lowi, Herbert Kaufman, Peter B. Clark, Robert E. Lane, Harold D. Lasswell, Karl W. Deutsch, and David Braybrooke. Two gifted and thoughtful sociologists, Robert O. Schulze and Robert A. Dentler, also contributed their time and talent, as did Francis E. Rourke, George M. Belknap, Newton D. Bowdan, Eugene N. Feingold, Micah H. Naftalin, Norton E. Long, Wallace S. Sayre, and H. Douglas Price. Marian Neal Ash of the Yale University Press assisted with her thoughtful and good-natured editorial advice.

This book was written with the help of a Brookings Research Fellowship in Governmental Studies, a Social Science Research Council Fellowship, a Falk Fellowship from the Political Science Department of Yale University, a faculty research grant from Wesleyan University, and gratuitous overpayments for token amounts of research from two indulgent patrons of political science, Peter H. Rossi and Robert Dahl. I also received the valuable stimulus of meeting with others engaged in community studies in all parts of the country at conferences in August 1957 and April 1960, under the auspices of the Social Science Research Council. In addition, I was permitted to work out some of my ideas in public. For permission to repeat a few thoughts here, I am grateful to the editors of

Social Forces, The American Sociological Review, The Journal of Politics, and *The Canadian Journal of Economics and Political Science.* *

A gesture of thanks is meager acknowledgment for the good humor and interest of members of my family—Edythe Polsby, Allen I. Polsby, and Daniel D. Polsby. This is also true of the occupant of the apex of my own personal power structure, Linda O. Polsby. Her work as research assistant, typist, proofreader, and thesaurus richly entitles her to the hope that I learn to write before Lisa S. Polsby learns to read.

My affection and gratitude for all these people persuades me to credit them with much of the merit of this book. On the other hand, pride of authorship forces me to claim exclusive responsibility for all faults and errors that remain.

N.W.P.

* "The Sociology of Community Power: A Reassessment," *Social Forces,* 37 (March 1959), 232–36; "Three Problems in the Analysis of Community Power," *American Sociological Review,* 24 (December 1959), 796–803; "How to Study Community Power: The Pluralist Alternative," *Journal of Politics,* 22 (August 1960), 474–84; "Power in Middletown: Fact and Value in Community Research," *The Canadian Journal of Economics and Political Science,* 26 (November 1960), 592–603.

Contents

Short Titles and Abbreviations

Am. J. Soc.	*American Journal of Sociology*
Am. Pol. Sci. Rev.	*American Political Science Review*
Am. Soc. Rev.	*American Sociological Review*
Baltzell, *Philadelphia*	E. Digby Baltzell, *Philadelphia Gentlemen* (Glencoe, Free Press, 1958)
Dahl, "Critique"	Robert A. Dahl, "Critique of the Ruling Elite Model," *American Political Science Review*, 52 (June 1958), 463–69
Dahl, *Who Governs?*	Robert A. Dahl, *Who Governs?* (New Haven, Yale University Press, 1961)
Hollingshead, *Elmtown*	August B. Hollingshead, *Elmtown's Youth* (New York, Wiley, 1949)
Hunter, *CPS*	Floyd Hunter, *Community Power Structure* (Chapel Hill, University of North Carolina Press, 1953)
Lynd, *M*	Robert S. Lynd and Helen M. Lynd, *Middletown* (New York, Harcourt, Brace, 1929)
Lynd, *MIT*	Robert S. Lynd and Helen M. Lynd, *Middletown in Transition* (New York, Harcourt, Brace, 1937)
Miller, "Industry and CPS"	Delbert C. Miller, "Industry and Community Power Structure," *American Sociological Review*, 23 (February 1958), 9–15
Schulze, "Bifurcation"	Robert O. Schulze, "The Bifurcation of Power in a Satellite Community," in Morris Janowitz, ed., *Community Political Systems* (Glencoe, Free Press, 1961)
Scoble, "Yankeetown"	Harry M. Scoble, Jr., "Yankeetown: Leadership in Three Decision-making Processes," read at the meetings of the American Political Science Association, September 1956

Warner, *Jonesville*   William Lloyd Warner et al., *Democracy*
                            in Jonesville (New York, Harper, 1949)
Warner, YC 1   W. Lloyd Warner and Paul S. Lunt, *The*
                            Social Life of a Modern Community, Yan-
                            kee City Series, 1 (New Haven, Yale Uni-
                            versity Press, 1941)
Warner, YC 2   W. Lloyd Warner and Paul S. Lunt, *The*
                            Status System of a Modern Community,
                            Yankee City Series, 2 (New Haven, Yale
                            University Press, 1942)
Warner, YC 3   W. Lloyd Warner and Leo Srole, *The Social*
                            Systems of American Ethnic Groups, Yan-
                            kee City Series, 3 (New Haven, Yale Uni-
                            versity Press, 1945)
Warner, YC 4   W. Lloyd Warner and J. O. Low, *The Social*
                            System of a Modern Factory, Yankee City
                            Series, 4 (New Haven, Yale University
                            Press, 1947)
Warner, YC 5   W. Lloyd Warner, *The Living and the*
                            Dead, Yankee City Series, 5 (New Haven,
                            Yale University Press, 1959)

COMMUNITY POWER AND POLITICAL THEORY

1. The Relevance of Political Theory to Community Power

It seems to be the unhappy fate of many of those who explore the intellectual roots of current writing in various areas of social science to suffer a certain amount of disillusionment with "old masters" in the field.[1] This book follows the pattern: it was begun as an inventory of knowledge about power in American communities, but now seeks primarily to criticize the approach which currently seems most influential in guiding research and to present an alternative. The literature of community power, which I had hoped would accumulate into a neat set of propositions constituting a reliable body of knowledge, presented unexpected problems.

These problems did not come about because the works I chose to study failed to agree among themselves. The major difficulty was, rather, to account for the extraordinary unanimity that scholars displayed in upholding certain propositions about community power—propositions which, according to a careful reading of the literature and independent research experience, seemed quite wrong.

Let me begin by expressing more precisely the sense in which I shall use the term "community power" and by identifying the body of knowledge under discussion. In its most general meaning, as far as social science is concerned, one can conceive of "power"—"influence" and "control" are serviceable synonyms—as the capacity of one actor to do something affecting another actor, which changes the probable pattern of specified future events.[2] This can be envisaged most easily in a de-

1. See, for example, David Easton, *The Political System* (New York, Knopf, 1953); Lawrence J. R. Herson, "The Lost World of Municipal Government," *Am. Pol. Sci. Rev.*, 51 (June 1957), 330–45; Stanley Hoffmann, "International Relations: The Long Road to Theory," *World Politics*, 11 (April 1959), 346–77; Herbert A. Simon, *Administrative Behavior* (2d ed., New York, Macmillan, 1957); Dwight Waldo, *The Administrative State* (New York, Ronald, 1948).

2. The term "actor" is meant to encompass individuals or groups of individuals acting in concert. Other proposed definitions of "power," most of them equivalent or identical to the one suggested here, may be found in the following sources: Robert Bierstedt, "An Analysis of Social Power," *Am. Soc. Rev.*, 15 (Dec. 1950), 730–38; Karl W. Deutsch, *Nationalism and Social Communication* (New York, Wiley, 1953),

cision-making situation. Where decisions are choices between alternative courses of action leading to outcomes A and B, an actor can be said to possess a certain amount of "power" if, by acting on others, he changes the comparative probability that these outcomes will take place. The amount of power the actor has in this situation is expressed by the magnitude of the changes he introduces.

This is clearly not all one might say about power. But at the moment it is important to observe that power as it is defined above can be applied to a host of social situations. Wherever two or more people engage in making decisions, or attempt to determine an outcome in any area of social life—whether, for example the family will go bowling or swimming, whether the company will promote Smith or Jones to Executive Suite, whether the nation will elect Nixon or Kennedy President—one can analyze the process of decision-making by making use of the notion of power. It is possible to distinguish three kinds of data with respect to decision-making which often serve as indices of the power of actors; one may ask (1) who participates in decision-making, (2) who gains and who loses from alternative possible outcomes, and (3) who prevails in decision-making. Identifying the last of these seems the best way to determine which individuals and groups have "more" power in social life, because direct conflict between actors presents a situation most closely approximating an experimental test of their capacities to affect outcomes. The other criteria are not especially useful in making interpersonal comparisons, though they often help to explain how and why certain alternatives are chosen. These indices make inferences about the exercise of power by actors possible, though hazardous.

This book is concerned primarily with decisions affecting large segments of the population of local communities, hence "community power," rather than "family power," "company power," or "national power." We shall be concerned primarily with local political power, since the political arena is the sector of community life in which large groups in the community make demands upon one another and collectively determine policy

pp. 46–59; Herbert Goldhamer and Edward Shils, "Types of Power and Status," *Am. J. Soc.*, 45 (Sept. 1939), 171–82; Harold D. Lasswell and Abraham Kaplan, *Power and Society* (New Haven, Yale Univ. Press, 1950); James G. March, "An Introduction to the Theory and Measurement of Influence," *Am. Pol. Sci. Rev.*, 49 (June 1955), 431–51; Felix E. Oppenheim, "An Analysis of Political Control: Actual and Potential," *Journal of Politics*, 20 (Aug. 1958), 515–34; Herbert A. Simon, "Notes on the Observation and Measurement of Political Power," *Journal of Politics*, 15 (Nov. 1953), 500–16. See esp. Robert A. Dahl, "The Concept of Power," *Behavioral Science*, 2 (July 1957), 201–15.

outcomes. We shall be examining answers to the question "Who rules?" in various American communities, that is, "who participates, who gains and loses, and who prevails in decision-making?" What criteria shall we use in evaluating answers to this question? It is necessary to consider provisionally the kinds of answers that have been made but are unacceptable, and the kinds of answers to be trusted. One very broad criterion can be stated at once. Findings that pretend to scientific acceptability must be verifiable. By this I mean two things. First, a verifiable answer must refer to events in the real world, accessible to more than one competent observer. Secondly, this answer must be put in such a form that in principle it is directly or indirectly subject to disproof by an appeal to evidence. If no evidence about the real world can possibly disprove a proposition, it can hardly be called scientific or empirical in character.

These are the essential, formal requirements for any scientific proposition.[3] It is also desirable, of course, that propositions actually be verified by observation—that is, that they be true; but this is an empirical rather than a formal requirement, and the latter concerns us here. Not all statements in science are propositions. Some statements used in scientific discourse propose linguistic conventions (definitions) and others propose provisional prescriptions about the relations between linguistic conventions and the real world (axioms). These statements, along with "primitive" terms, are necessary to scientific discourse. For example, only after stating a definition:

> Power is the capacity of one actor to do something affecting another actor, which changes the probable pattern of specified future events,

and an axiom:

> American communities may be divided into two groups (classes) which differ with respect to socioeconomic status,

can we arrive at a researchable proposition:

> The upper socioeconomic class has more power than the lower class.

For this latter statement to mean anything in a scientific sense, we must, according to the formal requirements postulated above, make refer-

3. See Morris R. Cohen and Ernest Nagel, *An Introduction to Logic and Scientific Method* (New York, Harcourt, Brace, 1934), p. 27: "A *proposition* may be defined as anything which can be said to be true or false." The view that a scientific proposition must be capable of disproof by appealing directly or indirectly to evidence about the real world is now widely accepted. However, the matter is by no means as simple as it sounds. See Karl R. Popper, *The Logic of Scientific Discovery* (New York, Basic Books, 1959), esp. pp. 40–43.

ence to specific decisions in which particular outcomes are affected by members of the classes into which we divide the population,[4] and, secondly, we must state the conditions under which we can take it as demonstrated that the upper class does not have more power than the lower class.

One of the themes of this book is that what social scientists presume to be the case will in great measure influence the design and even the outcome of their research. Suzanne K. Langer states this idea nicely when she says: "The way a question is asked limits and disposes the way in which any answer to it—right or wrong—may be given." [5] Another theme is that empirical presumptions entertained by many researchers in the field of community power exhibit certain characteristics in common. The illusion of unanimity in a large number of community studies is based on these family resemblances among presumptions, I suggest, rather than on adequate, repeated empirical demonstrations of patterns of community power.

I find it convenient to think of the empirical presumptions of researchers in community power as embryonic political theories, though this may stretch somewhat the conventional meaning of theory in science. Theory, as it is conventionally understood, consists of a number of logically ordered statements, asserting relationships among a number of events in the real world. Presumably "good" theory in science describes relationships among a relatively large number of real-world events using a relatively small number of hypotheses.[6] The political "theories" under discussion here can make no pretense to great simplicity, comprehensiveness, or internal consistency. However, they do perform perhaps the most important function of theory in social science; that is, they guide research.[7] It seems unnecessary after expressing this *caveat* to refer to "pseudo-theory," "pre-theory," or some such neologism.

4. Cf. Dahl, "Critique."

5. *Philosophy in a New Key* (New York, New American Library, 1948), p. 1. Robert K. Merton speaks of the "self-fulfilling prophecy" in social behavior but, curiously, not in social research. "The Self-fulfilling Prophecy" in Robert K. Merton, *Social Theory and Social Structure* (2d ed., Glencoe, Free Press, 1957), pp. 421–36. See also Karl Mannheim's treatment of the "total conception" of ideology: *Ideology and Utopia* (New York, Harcourt, Brace Harvest, 1936), passim.

6. See Cohen and Nagel, pp. 397–99, and Frank A. Pinner, "Notes on Method in Social and Political Research," in Dwight Waldo, ed., *The Research Functions of University Bureaus and Institutes for Government Related Research* (Berkeley, Bureau of Public Administration, Univ. of California, 1960).

7. See Robert K. Merton, "The Bearing of Sociological Theory on Empirical Research," and "The Bearing of Empirical Research on Sociological Theory," in *Social Theory and Social Structure*, pp. 85–117.

The particular political theory that seems to have been most influential in guiding current research on community power will be the primary object of attention in the immediately succeeding chapters. In focusing on this particular theory, and the findings it has produced, several other more or less self-contained bodies of knowledge, all of which deal directly in some way with community affairs, are ignored.[8] The decision to concentrate on contemporary studies of community power structures and their intellectual antecedents is made on the following grounds. First, these studies ask to be considered as "scientific" knowledge. Their authors implicitly accept the standards of verifiability suggested above, and it seems fair to judge them by application of these standards. Secondly, these studies are widely considered to have contemporary relevance to community affairs. They purport to explain currently observable patterns of community power. Thirdly, these studies include general statements about power in American communities. The community-as-a-whole is taken as the unit of study, and descriptions of intracommunity activities are systematically related to characterizations of the entire community. Thus we have some opportunity to compare units which are similar in the scope of their activities. Conclusions about communities may be regarded as grossly comparable with one another and as useful in interpreting findings in new communities. Finally, the works to be examined here cite one another conscientiously, and later studies give the strong impression that they have been shaped and guided by earlier contributions. Thus this is an on-going, self-conscious "scientific" literature, currently influencing the research concerns of workers in the field of community politics and power.[9]

What is the political theory contained in the literature to be examined in this book? The most general statement of the theory might be as follows: power is a subsidiary aspect of the community's social structure. "The political organization of Jonesville," writes one scholar, "fits the rest

8. Robert T. Daland has given an excellent bibliography of materials on urban politics, in which references to these bodies of knowledge may be found. Daland, "Political Science and the Study of Urbanism," *Am. Pol. Sci. Rev.*, 51 (June 1957), 491–509. See also Wallace S. Sayre and Nelson W. Polsby, "American Political Science and the Study of Urbanization" (mimeo., Committee on Urbanization, Social Science Research Council, July 1961). Focused more directly upon community power studies are two pamphlets containing, respectively, abstracts and summaries of substantial portions of the literature: Charles Press, *Main Street Politics* (East Lansing, Mich., Institute for Community Development, 1962), and Wendell Bell, Richard J. Hill, and Charles R. Wright, *Public Leadership* (San Francisco, Chandler, 1961).

9. In contrast, current textbooks in the field of city government appear not to exhibit several of these characteristics. See Herson, "The Lost World of Municipal Government."

of the social structure . . . curving or bulging with the *class outlines* of the body politic." [10] I am going to refer to this conception as a "stratification theory" of community power, since it suggests that the pattern of social stratification in a community is the principal, if not the only, determinant of the pattern of power.

Stratification studies make five assertions in common about power in American communities.[11]

The first proposition is:

1. *The upper class rules in local community life.*[12] Stratification studies differ in their descriptions of what constitutes the upper class. Some divide the classes on economic grounds, others according to status ascriptions by community residents. Some authors divide communities into two classes, others into five or six classes. Some authors hold that classes are "real" categories which are understood by citizens of the community and are used in their daily lives; others aver that classes are not real but rather are constructs convenient for analysis.[13] While these differences are

10. Warner, *Jonesville*, p. xviii. My emphasis.

11. There are, of course, occasional deviations from this list in isolated instances. Certainly the great majority of stratification studies uphold most of these assertions. Individual treatment of specific stratification studies, contained in Chapters 2 and 3, will make this clear.

12. Many community studies claim to have found this pattern. See: Lynd, *M* (see Short Titles and Abbreviations), pp. 47, 354, 374, 434, Lynd, *MIT*, pp. 74–75, 97, 377, 456, 459, and passim; Warner, YC 1, pp. 143–44, 168–73; Warner, YC 2, pp. 46–50; Baltzell, *Philadelphia*, pp. 32–35; Warner, *Jonesville*, pp. xviii, 100–02, 209, 294; Hollingshead, *Elmtown*, p. 72 and passim; Hunter, *CPS*, pp. 56, 62, 64, 79, and passim; Miller, "Industry and CPS," pp. 12, 13.

13. See, among other sources: Reinhard Bendix and Seymour Martin Lipset, eds., *Class, Status and Power* (Glencoe, Free Press, 1953); John F. Cuber and William F. Kenkel, *Social Stratification in the United States* (New York, Appleton, 1954); Kingsley Davis, *Human Society* (New York, Macmillan, 1949); Davis and Wilbert E. Moore, "Some Principles of Stratification," *Am. Soc. Rev.*, 10 (April 1945), 242–49; Hans H. Gerth and C. Wright Mills, *Character and Social Structure* (New York, Harcourt, Brace, 1953); Milton M. Gordon, *Social Class in American Sociology* (Durham, Duke Univ. Press, 1958); Gordon, "A System of Social Class Analysis," *Drew Univ. Bulletin*, 39 (Madison, N.J., Aug. 1951); Paul K. Hatt, "Social Stratification in the Mass Society," *Am. Soc. Rev.*, 15 (April 1950), 216–22; Hollingshead, *Elmtown*; Harold F. Kaufman, Otis Dudley Duncan, Neal Gross, and William A. Sewell, "Problems of Theory and Method in the Study of Social Stratification in Rural Society," *Rural Sociology*, 18 (March 1953), 12–24; Kurt B. Mayer, *Class and Society* (Garden City, Doubleday, 1955); Mayer, "The Theory of Social Classes," *Harvard Educational Review*, 23 (Summer 1953), 149–67; Harold W. Pfautz, "The Current Literature on Social Stratification: Critique and Bibliography," *Am. J. Soc.*, 58 (Jan. 1953), 391–418; Pfautz, "Social Stratification and Sociology," *Transactions of the Second World Congress of Sociology, 1953*, 2 (London, International Sociological Assn., 1954), 311–20; Baltzell, *Philadelphia*; William Lloyd Warner, Marchia Meeker, and Kenneth

important to the study of social stratification, they are side issues in the present context. *All* students of stratification agree that it is possible to talk about different classes in society. Although many assert that in principle communities can be stratified according to differences in the amount of power held by individuals,[14] all stratify communities on some basis other than power. It is these other bases for stratification that will concern us for a moment. These include income, occupation, housing, social participation, consumption patterns.[15] All of these are considered indices of social or economic standing, so it is proper to refer to the "upper class" as a group in the community of highest social-economic standing, without prejudice to any of the many different ways in which stratification writers arrive at their identification of this group. It is possible to suggest another formulation of this proposition: The group with the highest social-economic standing has the most power. If we can think of a "base" of power as a condition necessary for the exercise of power,[16] then we can state the proposition in still another way: a high social-economic position is the base of most community power.

Social stratification theory organizes individuals for analytical purposes into "strata," stacked one on the other. Thus stratification writers on community power see the upper class as at the top of a ladder of power, with others ranged below them. One of the most significant of the lower groups is composed of civic leaders and politicians, who are not themselves members of the upper class. Of these people, stratification writers assert:

2. *Political and civic leaders are subordinate to the upper class.*[17]

Subordination in two senses is implied or asserted in stratification studies of community power. Political and civic leaders as a group are said to possess less power than the upper class as a group, and in addition (or

Eels, *Social Class in America* (Gloucester, Mass., Peter Smith, 1957); Nelson N. Foote, Walter R. Goldschmidt, Richard T. Morris, Melvin Seeman, and Joseph Shister, "Alternative Assumptions in Stratification Research," *Transactions of the Second World Congress of Sociology*, 2, 378–90; Gerhard Lenski, "American Social Classes: Statistical Strata or Social Groups?" *Am. J. Soc.*, 58 (Sept. 1952), 139–44; Joseph A. Kahl, *The American Class Structure* (New York, Rinehart, 1957).

14. For example, Mayer, Gordon, Pfautz.

15. See Joseph A. Kahl and James A. Davis, "A Comparison of Indexes of Socioeconomic Status," *Am. Soc. Rev.*, 20 (June 1955), 317–25.

16. See Lasswell and Kaplan, *Power and Society*, p. 83.

17. For documentation among studies of specific communities, see Lynd, *M*, p. 434, and *MIT*, pp. 89, 321, 329, 334; Baltzell, *Philadelphia*, pp. 35, 364; Warner, Meeker, and Eels, *Social Class in America*, p. 13; Warner, *Jonesville*, pp. 97–101; Hollingshead, *Elmtown*, p. 86; Hunter, *CPS*, pp. 81–87, 93, 100, 162–63, 175; Miller, "Industry and CPS," p. 14; Delbert C. Miller, "Decision-making Cliques in Community Power Structures," *Am. J. Soc.*, 64 (Nov. 1958), 306–07.

perhaps as a consequence of having less power) they are held to take orders from or do the bidding of the upper class.

A third assertion of the stratification theory is:

3. *A single "power elite" rules in the community.*[18]

This constitutes an extension and elaboration of the propositions already expressed. We may think of an elite as a small group, always less than a majority of the community, and as a group selected by some means other than majority vote.[19] The upper class in every community studied fits these criteria. Another idea suggested by the term "power elite" is that the powers of the elite group are distributed over a large number of significant community decisions, so that stratification writers may say of the power elite that it stands at the apex of a pyramid of "all-purpose" power, dealing with a wide variety of community issues. This group is also held to be homogeneous in its social composition, being made up of members of the upper class.

Each of the various possible outcomes of issues may be said to allocate valued things and events in alternative ways. Stratification writers hold that it is in the interests of each class in society to increase its long-run share of values, but of course rulership implies that only one class possesses the means to accomplish this end. Hence the assertion of stratification writers that:

4. *The upper-class power elite rules in its own interests.*[20]

This arrangement, according to stratification writers, is not or at least should not be acquiesced to willingly by the other classes in society. The final characteristic of community power asserted in stratification studies is therefore that:

5. *Social conflict takes place between the upper and lower classes.*[21]

The reasoning here is that significant social conflicts follow the significant divisions of interest in the community, and these cleavages of in-

18. See Lynd, *MIT*, pp. 74–101; Baltzell, *Philadelphia*, pp. 364–71; Warner, *Jonesville*, p. 101; Hollingshead, *Elmtown*, pp. 72–73.

19. See Dahl, "Critique."

20. See Lynd, *MIT*, pp. 89, 99, 117, 321, 351; Warner, YC 1, p. 372; Warner, *Jonesville*, pp. 195–96; Hollingshead, *Elmtown*, pp. 123–24; Roland J. Pellegrin and Charles H. Coates, "Absentee-owned Corporations and Community Power Structure," *Am. J. Soc., 61* (March 1956), 413–19.

21. See Gerth and Mills, *Character and Social Structure*, pp. 339, 341; C. Wright Mills, "The Middle Classes in Middle-sized Cities," *Am. Soc. Rev., 11* (Oct. 1946), 520–29; Lynd, *MIT*, pp. 22, 25–44, 72, 91, 93, 329, 340, 360, 451, 452; Warner, YC 4, pp. 10, 66–89, 108–33, and passim; Warner, *Jonesville*, pp. 23, 107–08, 146, 197–98, 204; Hunter, *CPS*, pp. 247–48; Hollingshead, *Elmtown*, 123–24, 135, 451–52.

terest separate the community's upper from its lower social classes rather than divide other groups in the community whose members are recruited on some basis other than class memberships.

The two chapters immediately following present the case for and against these five propositions as it unfolds in the stratification studies of community power themselves. Chapter 4 discusses a separate empirical test of stratification theory, using findings for New Haven. Chapter 5 suggests possible explanations for discrepancies between assertions about community power found in the stratification studies and the facts of power revealed in a re-examination of the empirical materials. In Chapter 6, an alternative method for studying community power is outlined, and Chapter 7 sketches some tentative conclusions and hypotheses about patterns of power and decision-making in American communities.

A final introductory word about the fact that so many studies of community power have been heavily influenced by stratification theory. This is surely an interesting social fact in itself. For a long time, both stratification theory and community power were almost exclusively the province of sociologists. Power is conceived of by sociologists as one dimension of social life along which people may be stratified; hence power is of central interest to those engaged in mapping social structure and social change.[22] Political scientists have also traditionally concerned themselves with power and with the institutional order specialized to the exercise of political power in social life, the state.[23]

In recent years, however, political scientists have largely ignored power in American communities, and sociologists have undertaken to fill the gap in our knowledge about power in community life.[24] Thus, where one might have expected on the basis of disciplinary traditions that both sociologists and political scientists would have been busy analyzing power in American communities, the vast majority of the literature that constitutes current knowledge in the field is in fact the work of sociologists, and very little cross-disciplinary discussion seems to have occurred.

At least this was the case until recently. There are a great many signs of change. Sociologists are, if anything, increasing their research com-

---

22. Most current theoretical and textbook treatments of social stratification take this position. See the works cited in note 14 above.

23. See Easton, *The Political System*.

24. Several political scientists have made this point. See Herson, "The Lost World"; Daland, "Political Science"; and Herbert Kaufman and Victor Jones, "The Mystery of Power," *Public Administration Review, 14* (Summer 1954), 205–12.

mitments to community studies,[25] though it should be remembered that the community is a social laboratory of interest to sociologists for many reasons irrelevant to the study of power.[26] Political scientists, who seldom profess to a more important interest than the study of power, are now entering the field in force.[27] Most of these researchers seem acutely aware of their debt to recent sociological writings, though, for a variety of reasons, it seems likely that the gingerly acceptance originally accorded by political scientists to sociological findings will in time give way to more vigorous interdisciplinary criticism.[28] The most important factor in this change is no doubt the set of pluralist presumptions entertained by so many political scientists and outlined in Chapter 6 of this book.

It would be a great pity if disciplinary lines were to harden around the alternative political theories generated by stratification and pluralist presumptions.[29] Thus an attempt is made in this book to cross (if not

25. In the January 1959 issue of the *American Journal of Sociology*, numerous studies by sociologists of community leadership and politics were reported as in progress, pp. 405–15. See also Morton Rubin, "Report on 1961 Inventory of Research for the Committee on Community Research and Development, Society for the Study of Social Problems" (the Committee, 1961). This inventory of sociologists lists 63 separate projects, including 15 under the heading "Leadership, Decision-making."

26. There are, for example, ecological-demographic studies of communities (e.g. studies of land use and land values, and migration); studies of various other kinds of intracommunity events (e.g. crime rates); studies of individuals, using place of residence as a control (e.g. rates of student achievement in small-town versus big-city high schools); studies of community social-psychological states and changes (e.g. studies of community reactions to disaster).

27. Some of these studies are still unpublished. However, see Norton E. Long, "The Local Community as an Ecology of Games," *Am. J. Soc., 64* (Nov. 1958), 251–61, which draws on his experience in studying Boston; and Edward Banfield, *Political Influence* (New York, Free Press, 1961). Maurice Klain is studying community power and leadership in Cleveland, George Belknap has studied several cities in the San Francisco Bay area, Frederic Cleaveland and his students have re-examined community power in Atlanta, Aaron B. Wildavsky has a study of Oberlin, Ohio, in progress, and Benjamin Walter has studied three North Carolina communities. Benjamin Walter, "Political Decision-making in North Carolina Cities," *PROD, 3* (May 1960), 18–21. Other efforts, such as Harold Kaplan's study of Newark, are beginning to come out of the Metropolitan Study Program of Columbia University. See Sayre and Polsby for additional bibliographical information about this and other programs.

28. A good indication of the early success of sociological studies of power is the acceptance that Floyd Hunter's book, *Community Power Structure*, received upon its publication in 1953. Only Kaufman and Jones among political scientists expressed reservations about this work. See, in contrast, Daland, "Political Science and the Study of Urbanism," William J. Gore, and Fred S. Silander, "A Bibliographical Essay on Decision-making," *Administrative Science Quarterly, 4* (June 1959), 106, and reviews of the book by Louis Smith in *Journal of Politics, 16* (Feb. 1954), 146–50, and Donald S. Strong, *Am. Pol. Sci. Rev., 48* (March 1954), 235–37.

29. The temptation to engage in border warfare is perhaps understandable, but

straddle) disciplinary boundaries and to evaluate and compare the general scientific utilities of these alternative theories of community power.

there are at least two reasons why this should be resisted. First, and most obviously, it seems ridiculous for scholars thus to throw away chances to learn from one another. Secondly, the facts will not justify a general anathema directed across disciplinary lines; there are, as it happens, a goodly number of sociological pluralists, such as Seymour Martin Lipset, *Political Man* (Garden City, Doubleday, 1960); James S. Coleman, *Community Conflict* (Glencoe, Free Press, 1957); S. M. Lipset, Martin Trow, and J. S. Coleman, *Union Democracy* (Glencoe, Free Press, 1958); Peter H. Rossi, "Community Decision-making," *Administrative Science Quarterly, 1* (June 1957), 415–43; Arthur J. Vidich and Joseph Bensman, *Small Town in Mass Society* (Princeton, Princeton Univ. Press, 1958); James B. McKee, "Status and Power in the Industrial Community: A Comment on Drucker's Thesis," *Am. J. Soc., 58* (Jan. 1953), 364–70; Linton C. Freeman et al., *Local Community Leadership* (Syracuse, N.Y., Univ. College, Syracuse Univ., 1960).

There are also some political scientists whose work is heavily influenced by stratification theory. See, e.g., Robert E. Lane, *Political Life* (Glencoe, Free Press, 1959), pp. 256–75; Edwin Hoffman Rhyne, "Political Parties and Decision Making in Three Southern Counties," *Am. Pol. Sci. Rev., 52* (Dec. 1958), 1091–1107; Robert T. Daland, *Dixie City: A Portrait of Political Leadership* (University, Ala., Bureau of Public Administration, Univ. of Alabama, 1956); Andrew Hacker, "Liberal Democracy and Social Control," *Am. Pol. Sci. Rev., 51* (Dec. 1957), 1009–26; Hacker, "The Elected and the Anointed," *Am. Pol. Sci. Rev., 55* (Sept. 1961), 539–49.

Despite this blurring of lines it is undeniably the case that in large measure, each of the social sciences is a relatively independent, boundary-maintaining system, each with its own venerated ancestors, literature, training procedures, professional journals, and standards of relevance. Thus the chances are very much greater that subsequent research in community power will be influenced by stratification theory if the researcher is a sociologist, and by pluralist theory if he is a political scientist.

2. Research Consequences
of Stratification Theory (I)

In the preceding chapter, I presented five key propositions about power in American communities. I also indicated that in many studies of American communities these propositions have been given as presumbly accurate representations of social reality. In the present chapter and the one following I shall investigate the veracity of this claim.

Each of the five propositions is capable of being cast in the form of a hypothesis, of being proven or disproven by empirical evidence. The first question, then, is: Do these propositions correctly describe who rules in American communities—were the hypotheses actually verified by field research or were they, perhaps, empirically unsubstantiated deductions from basic axioms of stratification theory or "necessary" conclusions from the ideologies of researchers? As indications that a proposition has not been properly corroborated we can take the following symptoms: (1) data are given which tend to discredit or disprove a proposition, but the refutation of the proposition is never explicitly formulated; (2) the methods of a study either do not test hypotheses or permit premature confirmation by avoiding or by-passing direct tests; (3) refutations are recognized by authors as occurring in their data, but extraneous, ad hoc explanations are constructed, or extenuating circumstances claimed, so as to evade the necessity of giving up the propositions. The appearance of any single one of these three symptoms is sufficient to throw the findings of research into question. All three need not appear together. In the succeeding pages, I shall attempt to call attention to their appearance in stratification studies of power in eight American communities.

MIDDLETOWN (MUNCIE, INDIANA)

The oldest still-standing landmark among American community studies is the classic study of Middletown conducted by Robert and Helen Lynd in the middle 1920s and again in the mid-1930s.[1] Today, more than

1. Lynd, *M*, and Lynd, *MIT*.

a quarter-century after the Lynds began their pioneering work, the published reports of their findings repay many times over the attention of those interested in American community culture. The very great debt scholarship owes the Lynds is nowhere more apparent than in the frequency with which the Middletown books are cited in contemporary— even the most recent—research.[2]

This oldest of the stratification studies of community life is in many ways the best, since all five generalizations which seem to characterize stratification analyses of community power are set forth and accompanied by a wealth of circumstantial detail. Indeed, one of the Lynds' greatest contributions is the care and responsibility with which they recorded data that disproves each of the propositions of stratification theory, in spite of the fact that they themselves adhere to these propositions. This is, of course, the ultimate tribute to their skill as reporters.

They observed, for example, in the Middletown of 1925 that the "dominant interests" in the community were those of the "business class."[3] A decade later, the dominance of the business class had hardened into an "inner business control group" centering on, but not limited to, the "X" family. The power of this group was based on the "pervasiveness of the long fingers of capitalist ownership"[4] and "the economic life of the city"[5]—most particularly on the ability of this group to control the extension of credit.[6] Private business, in the Lynds' view, was the dominant institution of society,[7] and a "small top group" of "wealthy local manufacturers, bankers, the local head managers of . . . national corporations with units in Middletown, and . . . one or two outstanding lawyers" comprised the "business control group."[8]

Even in the 1920s businessmen tended to monopolize community prestige, at the expense of city political officials,[9] and when a member of the X family became a leader of the Democratic party in the 1930s,

2. See, for example, Milton M. Gordon, *Social Class in American Sociology* (Durham, Duke Univ. Press, 1958), chap. 3, esp. pp. 71–75; Kurt B. Mayer, *Class and Society* (Garden City, Doubleday, 1959), chap. 6; Miller, "Industry and CPS," pp. 9–15; Robert O. Schulze and Leonard U. Blumberg, "The Determination of Local Power Elites," *Am. J. Soc., 63* (Nov. 1957), pp. 290–96; Maurice R. Stein, *The Eclipse of Community* (Princeton, Princeton Univ. Press, 1960), esp. pp. 57–59.

3. *M*, pp. 354, 434, 476. The "business class" consisted of all those who made their living by addressing their activities primarily to *people:* 29% of the population of Middletown in 1920. The working class, those whose occupational activities were addressed to *things*, made up the remaining 71% of the population (*M*, p. 22).

4. *MIT*, p. 97.

5. *MIT*, pp. 74–75.

6. *MIT*, p. 456; *M*, p. 47.

7. *MIT*, p. 377.

8. *MIT*, p. 459.

9. *M*, p. 434.

the Lynds report, "local business control sat astride both parties." [10] The Lynds describe the typical city official as a "man of meager caliber" [11] and as "the man whom the inner business control group ignore economically and socially and use politically." [12]

> The professional politician in a city like Middletown occupies in reality a position somewhat apart. He is not ordinarily a person accepted in the inner councils of the business class, and yet he must work with it in order "to get anywhere." And, on the other hand, the business class have . . . little respect for local politics and politicians, viewing them as a necessary evil which business supports and controls only enough to ensure cooperation in necessary matters.[13]

The function of the politician, from the standpoint of the business class, is described still more explicitly:

> The inner business control group may meet and make their decisions as regards local politics in quite another setting, but it is here in these shabby smoke-filled poolrooms and cigar stores . . . that the small-time political lieutenants maintain their grip on the working class voters year in and year out.[14]

The Lynds report further that "the lines of leadership and the related controls are highly concentrated." [15]

> Middletown has . . . at present what amounts to a reigning royal family. The power of this family has become so great as to differentiate the city today somewhat from cities with a more diffuse type of control. If, however, one views the Middletown pattern as simply concentrating and personalizing the type of control, which control of capital gives to the business group in our culture, the Middletown situation may be viewed as epitomizing the American business-class control system. . . . The business class in Middletown runs the city.[16]

The Lynds enumerate the categories into which they divide their analysis of the totality of Middletown life: Getting a Living, Making a Home, Training the Young, Spending Leisure, Religion, Government, Caring

10. *MIT*, p. 329.
11. *MIT*, p. 89.
12. *MIT*, p. 321.
13. *MIT*, p. 329.
14. *MIT*, p. 334.
15. *MIT*, p. 99.
16. *MIT*, p. 77.

for the Unable, and Getting Information, and they find that in each category, the X family and the inner business control group dominated.[17] They quote, at the head of a chapter, this comment by a Middletown man, made in 1935:

> If I'm out of work, I go to the X plant; if I need money I go to the X bank, and if they don't like me I don't get it; my children go to the X college; when I get sick I go to the X hospital; I buy a building lot or house in the X subdivision; my wife goes downtown to buy X milk; I drink X beer, vote for X political parties, and get help from X charities; my boy goes to the X Y.M.C.A. and my girl to their Y.W.C.A.; I listen to the word of God in X-subsidized churches; if I'm a Mason I go to the X Masonic Temple; I read the news from the X morning newspaper; and, if I am rich enough, I travel via the X airport.[18]

The Lynds also observe that: "The control system operates at many points to identify public welfare with business class welfare." [19] In fact, members of the business control group "bother to inject just enough control over the confusion of local politics to insure a tolerable tax rate, support for 'sound' municipal cooperation in maintaining an open-shop town, control over the numerically dominant working class, and similar broad policies calculated to enable their central business of money-making to go forward without too much interference. And all of this is done by men like the X's with a strong sense of their actions being 'in the public interest.' " [20]

The inner business control group's notion of the public interest did not prevent them, the Lynds suggest, from "using relief expenditures to pull certain of their business chestnuts out of the fire," [21] or from making "interested 'deals' whereby the controls of the local *Realpolitik* are made to work in the interest of private interests or private interpretations of the public interest." [22]

One prominent example of such a "deal" was the sudden, unexpected increase by 50 per cent in the Middletown police force, following a decision by General Motors to quit Toledo, where their workers were on strike, and locate in Middletown *after*, it is alleged, the city administration pledged, "There will be no labor trouble in Middletown." The Lynds speculate on the effect of the request to increase the police de-

17. *MIT*, passim.
19. *MIT*, p. 99.
21. *MIT*, p. 117.

18. *MIT*, p. 74
20. *MIT*, p. 89.
22. *MIT*, p. 321.

partment's budget from $83,255 to $124,182 on Middletown's taxpayers
—"particularly . . . the working class." [23]

It puzzles the Lynds that conflict between the classes did not take
place more often in Middletown. They report "a common sense of direction" [24] among members of Middletown's top ruling elite, which they
contrast with the diffuse, disorganized, haphazard political stance of the
working class.

> Middletown labor . . . has no dynamic symbols for itself as *over
> against* the business class; but it has been taught by press, by school,
> by church, and by tradition to accept, as its own, watered versions
> of the official business-class symbols. . . . Unless there is a sharp
> rise in working-class solidarity in the interim, this Middletown
> working class, nurtured on business-class symbols, and despite its
> rebellious Roosevelt vote in 1936, may be expected to follow patiently
> and even optimistically any bright flag a middle-class strong man
> waves.[25]

The major arena in which the interests of the classes clashed in peace-
ful Middletown was in labor-management relations.[26] The Lynds describe
the lengths to which "business controlled local agencies" went to discourage an AFL organizer from attempting to unionize Middletown's
auto workers.[27]

> Middletown's controlling businessmen have always realized that
> such competitive advantage as their city possesses in the national
> market is traceable to its lower living costs and to its ability to mop
> up an "easy labor market" of corn-fed, unorganized American
> workers, willing to work for relatively low wages.[28]

Consequently, the "will of the business-class control mechanisms" [29]
was set against unionization. The Lynds indicate that these mechanisms
acted in two ways—to keep the city open shop and to coopt the working class. "Working in an open-shop city with its public opinion set
by the business class . . . workers do not readily segregate themselves
from the rest of the city." [30]

Nonetheless, the Lynds detect some indications of class cleavage, as
for example in local attitudes toward national politics[31] and in con-

23. *MIT*, p. 351.   24. *MIT*, pp. 91, 93.
25. *MIT*, pp. 454–55 (emphasis in original). See also pp. 367, 509.
26. *MIT*, pp. 25–44.   27. *MIT*, p. 37.
28. *MIT*, p. 36.   29. *MIT*, p. 28.
30. *MIT*, p. 26.   31. *MIT*, pp. 22, 360.

troversies over public sanitation[32] and shopping and school facilities.[33] They point also to obstacles on "the American ladder of opportunity." Workers in industries may no longer hope realistically to climb to the top, yet "in the past reality and the alleged permanent continuance of this universally accessible ladder lies the popular justification of the reigning *laissez faire* philosophy . . . As symbol and reality draw thus apart, the scene would seem to be set for the emergence of class consciousness and possible eventual conflict." [34]

The Lynds note one prominent exception to their claim that power in Middletown was in the hands of the economic elite. They observe that the Y family, almost as numerous and wealthy as the dominant X's, chose to withdraw from civic life and thus forfeit what one presumes would have been a position of power.[35] This immediately suggests that the Lynds recognize criteria other than the availability of financial resources as important in determining one's power position in the community. Civic participation appears also to be a criterion. However, as soon as a certain threshold of participation is reached, this criterion is ignored. The X family, for example, is represented as having diverse interests, most of them apolitical, but members of the family were active in both political parties.[36] The contents of these diverse participations are held to be unimportant, however. By asserting, though without supporting evidence, that the X's were guided by a "common sense of direction," the Lynds divest the criterion of participation of most of its utility.[37]

Other, more striking examples contradict propositions 1 and 2, which are, respectively, that the upper class rules, and political and civic leaders are subordinate to them. In these examples, the Lynds suggest the importance of Middletown's political organizations in determining policy outcomes even over the objections of the business class.

The first of these is the rejection of the sewage disposal plan.[38] A problem which literally pervaded the atmosphere throughout both Middletown studies was the dumping of factory wastes and other sewage into the White River. This river wound through the "nice" northern part of town, giving incongruous air to the pleasant upper- and middle-class homes situated there. On numerous occasions the North Side, represented by homeowners, leading business and professional people,

32. *MIT,* pp. 329, 340.
33. *MIT,* pp. 451, 454.
34. *MIT,* p. 72.
35. *MIT,* p. 91.
36. *MIT,* pp. 87, 91–93.
37. *MIT,* pp. 91, 93.
38. *MIT,* pp. 93, 121–22, 340 f.

the newspapers, and the Isaac Walton League, agitated to "keep White River white," but nothing was ever done about the problem because representatives on the City Council from the working-class section of town on the South Side saw no advantage to themselves and refused to authorize the expenditure of the necessary money. The issue arose again in 1935, when civic leaders succeeded in promoting a federal grant to help improve the sewage system, but even then the South Side refused to allow the bond issue which would have brought the city this improvement at bargain-basement prices.

Periodically members of the business class attempted to institute various kinds of political reform. Once they ran an able and attractive young businessman for mayor on a reform ticket. At other times they agitated for the city manager form of government. On every occasion, professional politicians succeeded in squashing this opposition, either by turning out large votes against the business-class proposals or by preventing them from appearing on the ballot.[39]

There are contradictions, too, of the third proposition, which implies that no difference can be discerned from issue to issue in the composition of the ruling elite. The Lynds mention numerous instances where small "special-purpose" minorities controlled certain areas of decision-making that were especially important to them, such as the "small minority" that cut the heart out of the Middletown library appropriation,[40] or the "small group" of businessmen who successfully opposed the elimination of dangerous railroad grade crossings.[41] Another example involved the Ku Klux Klan, which was originally brought to the city "by leading businessmen" as an anti-Democratic party organization. With the help of an outside professional organizer, the lower classes took the Klan over.[42] And there are the myriad instances recounted by the Lynds where administrators and functionaries of various of Middletown's public services—public health doctors, the township trustee, the Board of Safety, sanitation inspectors—refused to accept "overall coordination" in place of their accustomed autonomy.[43]

It can easily be seen that these examples also tend to disprove the fourth proposition, that the power elite rules in its own interests, since they indicate that at various times values were distributed in different

39. *M*, p. 427; *MIT*, p. 320.   40. *M*, p. 425.
41. *M*, p. 488; *MIT*, p. 320.   42. *M*, p. 481–82.
43. *M*, pp. 452, 455–56, 457, 466; *MIT*, p. 104. For other examples of "special-purpose" minorities, see *M*, pp. 423–25, 492; *MIT*, pp. 108, 113–14, 116, 130, 133, 395, 396, 461, 464.

ways to groups within classes, to lower rather than higher classes, and to groups cutting across class boundaries. A conspicuous example of the sharing of values across class lines was the situation at Middletown's community college. This school, say the Lynds, was run as a private satrapy by certain members of the X family, who gave the money to set it up. The X family retained an interest in the college through its memberships on the board of trustees, and they allegedly removed books from the library shelves and screened speakers who visited the campus.[44] But the presidency of this institution was apparently given to a nonelite politician as a payoff, in order to dissuade him from running for Congress.[45]

The notion that an upper-class power elite rules in its own interests rests on the presumption that the upper-class power elite in fact rules. We have seen that this describes only a part of the situation as reported by the Lynds. It may very well be that *when* the upper classes rule they do so in their own interests, although this is by no means a certainty. The Lynds assert, for example, that one of the areas in which the business class unequivocally held sway was in decisions pertaining to Middletown's Community Chest.[46] Most decisions taken by directors of the Community Chest were likely, however, to distribute some values disproportionately to members of the lower classes.

Another kind of decision remains to be considered in this connection: instances where nonelite members have a hand in distributing values to the upper classes. One can say that something like this took place when mass-scale unionization failed in Middletown. In spite of the fact that the business class intensely desired the defeat of the unions and actively mobilized to further this end, the Lynds report that three *other* factors defeated unionization in Middletown: the apathy of the workers, labor racketeering, and a hopelessly bungled effort at collective bargaining by incompetent union leaders.[47] In general, the business class is supposed to have reaped the benefit from the failure to organize open-shop Middletown, although the Lynds are at pains to point out both that the workers were not eager for unions and that unionization made headway in several small instances anyway.[48]

The evidence we have been considering also disproves the fifth proposition, which says that significant social conflict takes place exclusively

44. *MIT*, pp. 83–84.   45. *MIT*, pp. 216–17.
46. *MIT*, pp. 79, 139, 140. But see p. 142 where members of lower classes apparently distributed some forms of charity themselves.
47. *MIT*, pp. 28–33.   48. *MIT*, p. 33.

between the upper and lower classes. The Lynds describe conflicts within as well as between classes—for example, in their discussions of the "special-purpose" minorities, and in their description of the conflict between Middletown's real estate men and businessmen over a boost in taxes.[49] In contrast, it seems clear that class conflict in Middletown was anything but sharp.[50] This shows up particularly in Middletown's attitude toward national elections, where "local factories tried to exert a lot of pressure on their employees to vote Republican . . . The X glass plant practically forced employees to wear Landon buttons." [51] This might seem to indicate a business class united against the Democrats, but the Lynds document the fact that fully 46.8 per cent of the two-party vote in Middletown's *business-class* precincts went to Roosevelt in 1936, while working-class districts were giving Roosevelt a two-to-one majority.[52] The fact that Middletown went for Roosevelt in 1936 is to the Lynds an indication of a "rebellious" working-class vote,[53] but their own figures show that almost half the business class contributed to the rebellion.

For evidence of political rebelliousness, we would perhaps do better to inspect the extent of third-party Presidential voting, for the Socialists of Norman Thomas, William Lemke's right-wing Union party, and the Communist party. The number of Middletowners voting for any third-party candidate in 1936 was too small to provide more than a general suggestion of the distribution of rebels in the population. However, according to the Lynds' figures, a third-party vote for President was cast by one per cent of the voters in the business-class precincts, but only .7 per cent of the voters in working-class precincts.[54] While this should not be overinterpreted, it at least suggests that interclass cleavages and conflicts were relatively muted in the community.

It has already been noted that the Lynds grant that Middletown's workers seemed (to them abnormally) prone to avoid expressions of class antagonism. However, "real" conflicts apparently can take place, in the view of stratification analysts, without overt disagreement between alleged adversaries. Likewise "real" agreement is assumed to exist between Democratic and Republican members of the X family. For the moment, rejecting this presumption of "objectivity of interests," we may view instances of intraclass disagreement as intraclass conflict of in-

49. *MIT*, pp. 38–39.
50. The Lynds indicate this many times. For examples, see *MIT*, pp. 41, 448–49, 451, 453, 454, 503.
51. *MIT*, p. 361.   53. *MIT*, p. 509.
52. *MIT*, p. 359.   54. *MIT*, p. 359.

terests, and interclass agreement as interclass harmony of interests. To maintain the opposite seems perverse. If information about the actual behavior of groups in the community is not considered relevant when it is different from the researcher's expectations, then it is impossible ever to disprove the empirical propositions of the stratification theory, and they will then have to be regarded as metaphysical rather than empirical statements. The presumption that the "real" interests of a class can be assigned to them by an analyst allows the analyst to charge "false class consciousness" when the class in question disagrees with the analyst.[55] If we presume that the class is always wrong and the analyst invariably right when the two disagree, then there seems to be no way to disprove the analyst's empirical propositions by referring to the data his propositions are supposed to describe. Alternatively, if a decision to regard an action as "for" or "against" one's "real" class interests is not purely captious and personal, the researcher must provide us with some reasonably objective way of deciding the matter.

The most important observation to be made about the Lynds' presentation, then, is that their data never confront their working propositions. The presumption of objectivity of interests is one device by which this confrontation is avoided. Perhaps because the Lynds never state this presumption directly, they fail to appreciate its methodological consequences. But, more explicitly, the Lynds resort to an explanation of

55. As, for example, in *MIT*, p. 41. See also C. Wright Mills, "The Middle Classes in the Middle-sized Cities," *Am. Soc. Rev., 11* (Oct. 1946), pp. 520–29. Mills says:

"The general problem of stratification and political mentality has to do with the extent to which the members of an objectively defined stratum are homogeneous in their political alertness, outlook, and allegiances, and with the degree to which their political mentalities and actions are in line with the interests demanded by the juxtaposition of their objective position and their accepted values.

"Irrational discrepancies between the objectively defined bases of a stratum, the subjectively held policies of its members and their commonly accepted values do not necessarily point to problems of method. They may indicate the 'false consciousness' of the stratum we are examining."

In a footnote, he continues: " 'False consciousness,' the lack of awareness of and identification with one's objective interests, may be statistically defined as the deviant cases . . . for example, the rich who vote socialist, the poor who vote Republican. 'Objective interests' refers to those *allegiances and actions* which would have to be followed if the accepted values and desires of the people *involved in given strata situations* are to be realized." (Emphasis in the original.)

Note the presumption that "objective interests" exist; that there is a set of allegiances and actions which is appropriate for *all* members of a class. This presupposes a homogeneous set of "accepted values" for all class members. Secondly, Mills presumes that these particular allegiances and actions "have to be followed." This means in effect that a "best strategy" also exists. But are not these "objective" circumstances actually constructs of the analyst?

their data which may be identified as a variant of what Robert Merton calls the "and-also fallacy." [56] It will be remembered that the Lynds say of the "inner business control group" that they "bother to inject *just enough control* over the confusion of local politics to insure a tolerable tax rate, support for 'sound' municipal cooperation in maintaining an open-shop town, control over the numerically dominant working class, and similar broad policies calculated to enable their central business of money-making to go forward without too much interference." [57]

This formulation presents great difficulties to the outside observer. Any amount of evidence unfavorable to the view that the inner business control group rules can be discarded on the ground that the issues at stake were not essential for the maintenance of the power elite's position. The inner business control group only prevails on "important" issues, which are likely to be (by definition) those issues on which the inner business control group prevails. The only way out of this circle would be to apply criteria presented by the writers to distinguish important issues. But as long as this sort of explanation is resorted to, the Lynds' conclusions with respect to who rules Middletown cannot meet the standards of veracity previously proposed.

YANKEE CITY (NEWBURYPORT, MASSACHUSETTS)

William Lloyd Warner, in his monumental five-volume study of Yankee City, has little to say explicitly about power in the community.[58] However, his contribution to the study of communities cannot be ignored here because of its occasional use by other sociologists as corroborative evidence for the correctness of one or another of the five propositions. As Milton Gordon says, "a careful examination of his work will show that many aspects of the operation of community power controls appear in the studies and are related to position in the status structure." [59]

56. See Merton's comments in Paul F. Lazarsfeld and Robert K. Merton, "Friendship as a Social Process," in M. Berger, T. Abel, and C. Page, eds., *Freedom and Control in Modern Society* (New York, Van Nostrand, 1954), pp. 61–62.

57. *MIT*, p. 89. Emphasis supplied.

58. The Yankee City series includes the following titles: Vol. 1, W. Lloyd Warner and Paul S. Lunt, *The Social Life of a Modern Community* (1941); Vol. 2, Warner and Lunt, *The Status System of a Modern Community* (1942); Vol. 3, Warner and Leo Srole, *The Social Systems of American Ethnic Groups* (1945); Vol. 4, Warner and J. O. Low, *The Social System of a Modern Factory* (1947); Vol. 5, Warner, *The Living and the Dead* (1959). All were published in New Haven by the Yale University Press (see Short Titles and Abbreviations).

59. Gordon, *Social Class in American Sociology*, p. 95. See also, e.g., Bernard Barber, *Social Stratification* (New York, Harcourt, Brace, 1957), p. 67.

Warner never mobilizes data bearing directly upon the question of community power, except in a single chapter where he attempts to show (1) that the greater the importance of a city official the higher his social status, and (2) that members of the lower classes tended to be arrested by the police more often than upper-class members.[60]

Warner presents his findings on his first point in a figure (reproduced here) which he interprets in these words: "In summary, it can be said

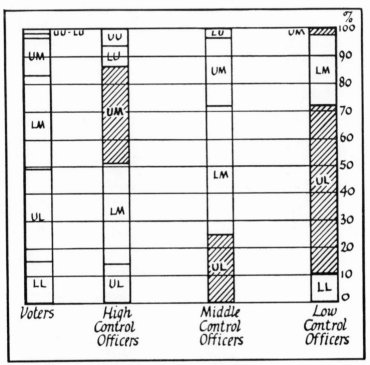

The Class Composition of the Officeholders and Voters
Source: Warner, YC 1, p. 370.

that the upper classes, together with the upper middle class, dominate the high control offices. They have a proportion of these offices far out of keeping with their representation in the general population." [61]

60. Warner, YC 1, pp. 366–78. Warner's second point is discussed below (p. 32) in connection with Hollingshead's similar observation.
61. Ibid., p. 372.

This chart deserves close examination, for it clearly shows that the "dominance" of the upper classes even in high control city government posts depended entirely upon their "togetherness" with the upper middle class. Since this dominance is unequivocally asserted by Warner, we may assume that Warner wishes to indicate by the chart that a coalition existed between certain adjacent classes. Assuming that coalitions are based on an expectation of common or complementary benefits and deprivations, we may infer from Warner's statement that the lower middle and lower classes did not share in the dominant coalition and hence may be presumed to have enjoyed noncomplementary, that is, different, benefits and deprivations from policy outcomes. Thus Warner indirectly asserts the propositions of the stratification theory which hold that upper classes are politically separated from those beneath, and in competition rather than in alliance with them in decisions allocating scarce resources —such as public office—in the community.

Other indications of conflict and divergence of interest appear in the Yankee City volumes. For example, Warner discusses at length an incident illustrating "how a very small number of upper class people can control the large number from the lower ranks." [62] In this incident the candidate supported by upper-class members of a community fraternal organization, the Veterans of All Wars, was elected president of the group.[63] Upper-class members of the organization became interested in the election after upper-class ministers asked them to put a stop to the importation by the organization of burlesque dancers from Boston. Warner indicates, in his description of this election, that upper-class members, in influencing the outcome in their favor, had at stake a certain special interest in the election, namely, the protection of the status reputation of Yankee City—an indulgence which could be expected to accrue largely to their own benefit.[64]

The first proposition of the stratification theory states that the highest group in terms of social-economic standing is also the most powerful group in the community. Thus, in Yankee City, according to Warner, "The Yankees are the most powerful group in the city, but the ethnics each year increase their power and prestige while they shed their variant mores and accept those of the dominant Yankees." [65] However, Warner makes clear that not *all* Yankees were members of the Yankee City ruling elite; the "solid, highly respectable upper-middle class," which was 81.2

62. Ibid., p. 198.
63. Ibid., pp. 143–44, 168–73; YC 2, pp. 46–50.
64. Ibid., p. 172.   65. Warner, YC 4, p. 3.

per cent Yankee,[66] is described as "the people who get things done and provide an active front for the classes above them." [67] The provision of an "active front" was, of course, anticipated in the second key proposition.

Finally, what of social conflict between the classes? Warner describes several such conflicts in Yankee City. For example, upper-class members got an injunction to prevent a factory near their homes from performing night work. The owner of the factory, miffed, moved his operation out of the community, throwing 120 lower-class workers out of jobs. This occasioned much interclass resentment, it is alleged.[68] Warner also reminds us frequently of the latent struggle between the classes inherent in the Veterans of All Wars election.

These were of relatively small magnitude, compared to the major strike in which all the workers in Yankee City's principal industry walked off their jobs.[69] This Warner sees as a conflict between the classes exacerbated (if not precipitated) by two factors: blocked mobility for workers within the factory[70] and the acquisition of the factories by absentee owners who were removed from social constraints which the community might have employed on hometown owners.[71]

Warner says: "Manufacturers associations have been formed without public resistance, but labor unions have been resisted both by management and by some sectors of the general public. This dual development reflects the increasing seriousness of the conflict of interests between the different grades which has accompanied the increasing social distance between them." [72]

Data contrary to the five key propositions, which Warner clearly supports, may be found throughout the Yankee City studies, though they are never recognized as such. For example, Warner gives tacit recognition to the vote as a base of power in Yankee City when he discusses

a Yankee City mayoralty election when the only candidates were two Irishmen—Kelly [Upper-Lower] and McCormack [Upper-Middle]. The former conducted his campaign largely by castigation of Hill Street [rich people] for its iniquities to the poor of River Street and to the small taxpayers. He won the election easily, apparently

66. Warner, YC 2, p. 74. In this class are included 7,787 Yankees, while 3,813 Yankees are assigned to the classes above the upper middle.

67. W. Lloyd Warner, Marchia Meeker, and Kenneth Eels, *Social Class in America* (Gloucester, Peter Smith, 1954), p. 13.

68. Warner, YC 4, p. 10.

69. Ibid., passim.

70. Ibid., pp. 66–89.

71. Ibid., pp. 108–33.

72. Ibid., p. 122.

carrying the entire vote of the two lowest classes, both native and Irish, and at least half the votes of the lower-middle class. Even the lower-lower class native descendants of the old fisherman group, who traditionally "hate" the Irish, lined up the two candidates and decided that Kelly looked less Irish than did McCormack and so they voted for him (Kelly). Actually, Kelly conformed far more to the conventional conception of the Irish physical type than did McCormack . . .

McCormack, on the other hand, was strongly supported by members of the three highest classes, native as well as Irish, and had this to say to the interviewer; "When I ran for mayor the last time I don't think that more than two out of every ten Catholics voted for me. I think the other eight voted for Kelly, and most of the votes I got were from the Protestants." [73]

In an indication that groups other than classes may have had significance in community politics, Warner also mentions that the Negroes, Poles, and Greeks of Yankee City were socially homogeneous and politically active.[74]

Warner does not assert that Yankee City politicians subordinated themselves to economic and status leaders: he claims, after all, that they tended to have power commensurate with their status. But in the election campaign just described, the higher-status people were unable to achieve the election of the less obnoxious of two Irishmen running for mayor. This defeat of the relatively united upper classes is one aspect of Yankee City life not accounted for in the five propositions. And what happens when the upper classes are split? Such a division actually occurred in the single most significant social conflict to take place in Yankee City during Warner's research project. When the workers in Yankee City's shoe mills struck, Yankee City merchants backed the laborers against management.[75] So did the mayor and the police.[76] The workers won the right to bargain collectively and achieved the establishment of new wage and work standards.

73. Warner, YC 3, p. 94.
74. Ibid., pp. 263–64, 268–69, 276–78; Warner, YC 2, p. 82. It is well to remember in this connection that one of the criteria which originally led Warner to pick Yankee City was the apparent dominance of Yankees in the life of the town, Warner, YC 1, pp. 5, 38. And, indeed, "natives" made up over half of Yankee City's population of 17,000, leading every other ethnic group in five of Warner's six "classes." They were outnumbered only in Warner's upper-lower class, where the Irish were found to predominate, Warner, YC 2, p. 74.
75. Warner, YC 4, p. 44.   76. Ibid., pp. 34, 43, 146.

The outcomes of these conflicts directly contradict the notion that the upper classes invariably prevail; and the split in upper-class sympathies also casts doubt on the homogeneity of class positions and on the allegation that conflicts customarily pit the classes against one another.

The Yankee City books do not take up the question whether or not there was a single power elite. Warner discusses only two conflicts at length; the relatively trivial Veterans of All Wars election and the very significant city-wide strike. Certainly different people participated and prevailed in each instance, thus justifying a suspicion that decision-making in Yankee City was more fragmented than stratification theory normally allows.

Warner insists, in interpretive remarks, that the lower classes did not "really" win the great strike. He conceives of the advent of unions as an admission by workers that they no longer may rise to the top occupationally in the American tradition. While Warner grants that there may be certain mitigating changes in the American economic structure, he believes that "essentially the same basic relations of power and prestige will continue and, from all present indications, increase in strength; and the social distance between the top and bottom will be extended." [77]

One cardinal assumption is at the base of this prognosis, namely, that all men strive (or should strive) to reach "the top." [78] The top is described as a windswept plateau attained by only a few men, and then only at the expense of others; a place where community status and power are concentrated. This conception has been called the "lump of power" fallacy and criticized on the ground that power should not be conceived of as a "thing," limited in amount and located by definition in any particular place in the social structure. [79] Once power is defined as Warner proposes, there is no possible appeal to facts and no way to discover that power is exercised by those originally excluded in the terms of the definition.

Yankee City's workers, among others, were so excluded. Not being on "the top," nor even, in general, upward mobile in their social status, how could they possibly constitute a powerful social group? Warner's own account of the strike leaves us with the inescapable impression that they were indeed very powerful in Yankee City, but his analysis

77. Ibid., p. 189.
78. Ibid., p. 194. This theme runs through many of Warner's books; cf. his *American Life: Dream and Reality* (Chicago, Univ. of Chicago Press, 1953), pp. 103–23.
79. Cf. Charles E. Lindblom, "In Praise of Political Science," *World Politics, 9* (Jan. 1957), 240–53, esp. 251.

takes no inventory of the range and bases of this power, the techniques through which it was exercised, or the prerequisites and consequences of its exercise in the community.

ELMTOWN-JONESVILLE (MORRIS, ILLINOIS)

Two separate studies were concurrently made of Morris, a small town in northern Illinois, in the late 1930s and early 1940s. W. Lloyd Warner called the community Jonesville, and August B. Hollingshead called it Elmtown.[80] The major purpose of both studies was to establish empirically the connection between ascribed social status and various kinds of social participation.

Hollingshead's research centered around the high school. He discovered that the social status of students' families made significant differences in the school attendance records of children, in their nonathletic participation, their marks, and the ways in which discipline was applied to them.[81] The comments I shall make, however, deal only with the question of who "controlled" the community, which Hollingshead also discusses.

Hollingshead quotes at length an informant who describes power in Elmtown in these words:

> It's an aristocracy of wealth, nothing else . . .
>
> The inner circle of top aristocrats is made up of people who have a close community of interest. They all have property and a good income. They run around in pretty closely knit groups, and it's mighty hard for a stranger to break into one . . . Most of the husbands are dead now, but the women still play Whist and 500. That's the most powerful group in town . . . This is the group that can really put on the pressure. They own a lot of interests, land, town property, the banks and other things, and they have great prestige and power.[82]

The issues on which the "inner circle of top aristocrats" were powerful are not specified in detail, but apparently ranged over a wide array of matters. Hollingshead's informant says of this group:

> When they want something done, they bear down on their children, in-laws, relatives and grandchildren. If voting's involved, they let their tenants and employees know how they feel. When an issue

80. Warner, *Jonesville*; Hollingshead, *Elmtown*. See Short Titles and Abbreviations.
81. Hollingshead, *Elmtown*, pp. 129, 169–70, 180–92.
82. Ibid., p. 72.

comes up, I can see this crowd pull together. I've seen them take sides on so many issues. I can just about tell ahead of time how they'll line up . . . When I want something, I always go to this group . . . If I can't get them on my side I drop the idea.[83]

In discussing the relationship between "Class I" families—those of "wealth and lineage"—and political leaders, Hollingshead says:

Large tax bills accompany extensive ownership: consequently these Class I families have a direct interest in keeping assessments and tax rates low. They accomplish this effectively, within the community and the county, through the control of the two major political party organizations on the township and county levels.[84]

The Elmtown school board is described as consisting of:

Middle aged business and professional men from the top two classes who possess a highly developed sense of responsibility to these classes especially with respect to the preservation of economic interests, power and prestige. The policies they have followed in the administration of the school system have reflected the community interests of their own social classes, and, to a less extent, those of the little business and professional people in the lower middle class.[85]

The school board believed that only those high school children who could "profit from a high school education" should use the public facilities. "In general, they mean the sons and daughters of the three higher classes, and those in Class IV, if they 'behave themselves.' Adolescents in Class V are not considered to have enough ability to 'profit from a high school education.'"[86]

Hollingshead says that local school board elections were "carefully controlled" so as to elect "conservative men who have represented through the years the political, economic, social and educational interests of classes I and II *rather than* the other four-fifths to seven-eighths of the population."[87] The only instance in recent history where the school plant was materially improved came, says Hollingshead, in the "early 1920's, after a terrific struggle between the 'better families' and the 'laboring class.'"[88]

83. Ibid., pp. 72–73.   84. Ibid., p. 86.
85. Warner, *Jonesville*, p. 195 (in a chapter by Hollingshead).
86. Ibid., p. 196.
87. Hollingshead, *Elmtown*, pp. 123–24. Emphasis supplied.
88. Ibid., p. 135.

However, Hollingshead indicates that conflicts were rare. Most Elm-towners, he says, took the "control of community institutions by the upper classes" as "natural." This upper-class control, says Hollingshead, "tends to result in the manipulation of institutional functions in the interests of individuals and families who have wealth, prestige, and power," and this in turn "guarantees the continuation, into the indefinable future, of the class system and its inequalities." [89]

Four kinds of evidence are proposed to substantiate the claim that Elmtown's social "Class I" constituted the community's power elite. First, Hollingshead makes a series of compelling observations on the relationship between class and law enforcement. Hollingshead says of Class I people: "Some of them may not observe the laws of the community with care, yet there are no arrests." [90] Lower down on the scale, arrests and convictions were more frequent. Four per cent of Class III and 14 per cent of Class IV fathers were convicted in local courts of offenses between 1934 and 1941, and, for Class V, the comparable figure rose to 46 per cent. [91] It will be remembered that Warner made the same point in his study of Yankee City.

How does this relate to power in Elmtown? Hollingshead seems to be saying that the law was enforced differently on different classes. It is implied that crime occurred randomly throughout the population, but immunity from arrest was a peculiar perquisite of high status and, therefore, an indication of power. [92] The question is perhaps more complicated than Hollingshead's presentation reveals. In weighing the significance of the statistics, we should perhaps take account of (1) the possibility that owing to the unfavorable conditions of life generally present among the lower classes—conditions vividly described by Hollingshead—the lower classes would actually commit most of Elmtown's crimes; (2) the possibility that the two highest classes, comprising a few, very small, intensively interacting, "respectable" cliques, were in fact severely constrained by the circumstances of *their* lives from committing crime. In one sense, perhaps Hollingshead's findings on this point argue that communities produce characteristic "rational" patterns of deviance from legality as surely as they produce patterns of acquiescence. [93]

89. Ibid., pp. 451–52.
90. Ibid., p. 89.
91. Ibid., pp. 110, 119–20. The reference presumably is to fathers of the high school students whom Hollingshead studied closely.
92. Hollingshead says this explicitly on p. 79.
93. Cf. Robert A. Dentler and Kai T. Erikson, "The Functions of Deviance in Groups," *Social Problems*, 7 (Fall 1959), 98–107.

Both the social meanings of arrest and opportunities to commit offenses differ greatly between the top and bottom of the status pyramid. Immunity from arrest no doubt means a great deal more to members of the upper class than to those at the bottom—except possibly those lower-class members engaged for livelihoods in illicit occupations. In this connection it is important to note that Elmtown's most illustrious bawdy house, Polish Paula's, catering to a lower-class clientele had "not been raided for a quarter of a century." [94]

Although respectability is perhaps a necessary condition of high community-wide prestige, no one, I think, will argue that it is a necessary condition of power[95]—and Hollingshead does not actually say this though he implies it. By demonstrating, then, the relative proneness to arrest of the lower classes, Hollingshead has not demonstrated that they were powerless.

The second point made by Hollingshead to substantiate his claim that the upper classes controlled community policies is that they controlled the two major party organizations.

> The candidates for public office, except the district attorney and the judge, are generally not members of Class I, but this does not mean that they are free of controls exerted by Class I interests. Money, legal talent, and political office are instruments used to translate interests into effective power. They are relied upon to implement decisions in contests which involve raising tax bills through public improvements, such as new public buildings, schools, roads or welfare programs. This behind-the-scenes control results in the formulation of conservative policies and the election of officials who act in the capacity of agents for Class I interests.[96]

This argument from evidence bears a resemblance to Hollingshead's argument that the law was enforced unequally upon the classes in that in both cases "real" power was held "behind the scenes," and was ex-

94. Hollingshead, *Elmtown*, p. 79. At this point in his book, Hollingshead seems to suggest that power is *not* an epiphenomenon of status. He never reiterates this opinion, however, and I take the very much more numerous statements such as those quoted previously in this chapter as more representative of his position.

95. For discussion and examples bearing on this point, see Robert K. Merton, "Social Structure and Anomie," in Merton, *Social Theory and Social Structure* (Glencoe, Free Press, 1957), pp. 131–60; William F. Whyte, *Street Corner Society* (Chicago, Univ. of Chicago Press, 1955), pp. 194–252. See also the Lynds' description of George R. Dale, the mayor of Middletown, who was elected to office after serving a term in jail, *MIT*, pp. 322–27.

96. Hollingshead, *Elmtown*, p. 86.

ercised covertly through "agents." The general argument of covertness in power exercise is often met with in stratification studies of community power and may be said to take two characteristic forms. The first maintains simply that there is a power-holding group behind the scenes though the characteristics of the group are not specified in detail. Researchers who are led to reject on empirical grounds the notion that a *specific* group is in fact the covert power elite can be said to have failed to disprove the proposition because there may be some *other* group which performs this function. This is the "principle of infinite regress" described by Dahl.[97] It effectively bars empirical research from contributing to the discussion of community power.

A variant of this principle appears quite frequently in stratification studies, including Hollingshead's work, as we have seen. In the case of *Elmtown's Youth,* it is not the identity of the ruling group which is left to the imagination, but rather the *means* by which the group controlled. The argument that the social-economic elite ruled Elmtown covertly means, in effect, that all overt manifestations (i.e., those observable by the researcher) of powerlessness or indifference on the part of this group are to be ignored in favor of the presumption that they were in fact secretly in control of community affairs. Once again, the findings of research are prevented from interfering with the description of social reality proffered by the author.

In the case of Hollingshead's second argument, as with the first, the evidence is by no means clear in support of the five key propositions. Warner's *Democracy in Jonesville* provides us with more detailed information about the political organization of the community, greatly supplementing Hollingshead's presentation. Little information is given about government office-holders, but the party organizations responsible for nominations and elections are described in some detail. Five of Elmtown's six Republican precinct committeemen were members of Class IV. The sixth, representing the "silk stocking" district, was a member of Class II.[98] The Republican party normally dominated Elmtown politics. Its "behind-the-scenes" leaders were three in number: an elderly Irish, Roman Catholic judge; the young editor of the newspaper; and a rich attorney with good connections in state-house Republican circles.[99] Joseph Rosenstein, the author of the political chapter in the Warner volume, makes it clear that these three men had practically no policy preferences and that they competed with one another for private power

97. Dahl, "Critique," 463–69.   98. Warner, *Jonesville,* p. 231.
99. Ibid., pp. 226–31.

within the party organization.[100] The Republican party organization, owing to long-standing lack of unity among its "big shots," was held to be a relatively unorganized machine.[101] The main beneficiaries of the organization were said to be the precinct committeemen, who were rewarded with state patronage when Republicans were in control in state politics.[102]

The Democratic party, too, had been "beset by personal rivalries and factional difficulties." [103] The Democrats subsisted almost entirely on federal and state patronage during the years studied.

> Locally, the Democratic party is poor in resources—poor in terms of friends of the party who have money to contribute, and poor in terms of voters with Democratic traditions.[104]

The Republicans, in spite of their own factional warfare, had succeeded in gaining a strong majority position in the community.

> Financial strength at the top is complemented by the skill with which the Republican party has cultivated the voters of all classes and religious groups over a period of years . . . Today . . . large numbers of Catholics participate in the party as voters, and ambitious Catholic politicians find that the party is open to them. Among the various classes, too, the Republican party has been successful in establishing itself. The top positions of leadership go to men of the upper and upper middle classes—men who have the social skills and contacts to establish the proper "outward" relations in the party, and to maintain the local relationships demanded of leaders in the party [i.e. (apparently) in order to get financial backing from the upper classes]. But, as the statistical materials show, staunch friends of the Republican party are found in all classes. People farther down in the class system vote Republican, not only because of family tradition and social and economic pressures in the community, but also because their participation is actively solicited by the "wheel horses" of the party—men who generally come from lower classes . . . The efficient activities of these wheel horses can be traced partly to their own zeal for the party, but that zeal is reinforced by more tangible rewards—jobs and campaign money which, in turn, it is the function of the local "big shots" to ensure.[105]

100. Ibid., pp. 230–31.   101. Ibid., p. 228.
102. Ibid., p. 225.   103. Ibid., p. 233.
104. Ibid., p. 234.   105. Ibid., pp. 234–35.

A careful reading of these words suggests that in claiming upper-class control of the parties Hollingshead has mistakenly assumed that the members of a status layer have the same political interests, that they effectively unify themselves in pursuit of these interests, and that this takes place at the expense of other status groups. According to the account in the Warner book, party leaders were in general apathetic about policy, were not united, and their activities generated benefits for members of many status groups.

The third bit of concrete evidence Hollingshead advances in favor of Class I domination has to do with the selection of the Board of Education. He describes in detail the process by which prosperous, male, Protestant Republicans were selected for the board by the predominantly upper-class leaders of the Rotary Club. Hollingshead says:

> When a vacancy is to occur, the selection of a man for the Board of Education is left to the President of the Board. He discusses possible candidates with his friends on the Board and in the Rotary Club. Generally, he invites a fellow Rotarian with whom he believes he can work to become a candidate. The President then files this man's name with the election clerk; nothing is said publicly about the impending vacancy or the forthcoming election until after the last date for filing has passed. Then *The Bugle* runs a news item stating that the date for filing names for the school election has passed, that such-and-such men have filed as candidates for the Board of Education, and that Mr. X has filed again for President of the Board. Little additional publicity is given to the election until *The Bugle* carries the necessary legal notices of the polling places and names of the candidates. On election day, only a handful of voters go to the polls to elect the hand-picked candidates. In 1940, 132 votes were cast; in 1941, 114, and in 1942, 84.[106]

How can we account for the success of these maneuvers? How, for example, could a board member's intention to resign be kept a secret in Elmtown? As Hollingshead says:

> In a town of 6,000 people, everything that is done, or not done, and then talked about, tends to be personalized. One person does something at some time; other persons know about it, find out about it, and above all gossip about it, and then pass judgment on it.[107]

106. Hollingshead, *Elmtown*, p. 123.   107. Ibid., p. 44.

The Elmtown school board's term of office was set by statute, and all seven members of the board stood for election at the same time. Anyone could be placed on the ballot for election to one of the seven non-paid, nonpolitical positions on the board by filing a petition signed by 50 voters, or by 10 per cent of the voters in the last school election, whichever was less. These basic facts were at the disposal of the public, if the public wanted to take notice of them.[108]

But, apparently, interest in elections to the Board of Education was exceedingly low, judging from Hollingshead's figures on turnout. The machinations depicted above seem likely to have assured control over the board by a small group in a situation where no other group cared to contest the matter, but we should not assume that some seriously competing group could easily have been prevented from trying to fill vacancies—or nonvacancies—on the board. Finally, we should be wary of concluding that this method for selecting board members necessarily predicts anything about the policies of the board in the conduct of its business.[109]

Hollingshead indicates that Class I and II dominance on the board would make such a prediction possible. But his discussion of a spectacular conflict over the physical condition of the public high school casts grave doubt on this proposition. This introduces the fourth kind of empirical evidence bearing on the propositions of the stratification theory. The important facts of the situation seem to have been the following.[110]

The high school, owing to an obsolete plant, lost its accreditation. Some members of the Board of Education were shocked and launched an investigation, which resulted in numerous minor repairs to the building. A new high school was clearly necessary, Hollingshead believes. It proved impossible, however, to raise money in Elmtown for this purpose.

Hollingshead attributes to Class I influence the failure of the Board of Education to build a new high school. The land in Elmtown's school district was largely in the hands of Class I people, and taxes on the land formed the main source of income for school purposes. The members of

108. A letter to me from the office of the principal of the Morris High School in September 1959 gives this current information about the laws pertaining to the election of the school board. This letter also states that, aside from minor changes in the election code, the basic facts given were the same when Warner and Hollingshead did their research in Morris some twenty years ago.

109. On this point see especially the excellent review of the literature contained in W. W. Charters, Jr., "Social Class Analysis and the Control of Education," *Harvard Educational Review*, 23 (Fall 1953), 268–83, esp. 271–72.

110. Hollingshead, *Elmtown*, pp. 132–40, 142–47.

Class I did not want their taxes raised; *therefore* nothing "serious" was done about the school.

However, Hollingshead mentions in passing that the last time any improvements were made in the community's educational plant, the vote of the "laboring class" made them possible.[111] The very element lacking in the more recent situation described by Hollingshead was an aroused populace. Despite repeated invitations to visit the school, no parents availed themselves of the opportunity.[112] Classes III, IV, and V, containing the vast majority of Elmtown's population, are described by Hollingshead as apathetic on the school issue. Class I opposed school improvements for personal financial reasons. Who in the community favored school improvements? Many members of Class II, says Hollingshead, most conspicuous among them leaders of the Board of Education.[113] But if this were the case, then it could not also be true that the Board of Education was a tool of Class I. That is, in the only community-wide conflict having to do with schools, the Board of Education seems to have opposed the "moneyed interests."

It is still true that the large landholders won their battle—at least temporarily—to hold the line on taxes. Hollingshead does not detail the techniques they used in securing their victory. But it does seem important to note that this victory was not won covertly but openly and by majority rule at the polls, where the voters rejected a proposed bond issue to build a new high school.[114]

Power relations in Jonesville are described by W. Lloyd Warner as a product of the community's main social cleavage, which separated management from workers in "The Mill" where better than a third of all Jonesville's urban workers had jobs. Not surprisingly, Warner says that the Mill dominated the town:

> When the citizens of the town talk about The Mill, they rarely refer to it in economic terms but speak in moral terms of its place in the life of the town. They are forever concerned with its power for good and evil in the lives of Jonesville.
>
> The economic and social force of The Mill affects every part of the life of the community. Everyone recognizes its power. Politicians, hat in hand, wait upon Mr. Waddell, manager of The Mill, to find out what he thinks on such important questions as "Shall the tax rate be increased to improve the education our young people are

111. Ibid., pp. 135–36.   112. Ibid., p. 136.
113. Ibid., pp. 139, 142–47.   114. Ibid., p. 139.

getting?"—"Shall the new minister be Mr. Jones or Mr. Smith?"—"Should the city support various civic and moral enterprises?"—"Should new industries enter the town and possibly compete with The Mill for the town's available labor supply?" They want to know what Mr. Waddell thinks. Mr. Waddell usually let them know.[115]

The Mill management is said to be opposed to other industries' coming into town and to have taken steps to prevent new plants' opening up and creating competition in the labor market. Several informants reaffirmed the following statement of a person who knows the town intimately: "The people out at The Mill are very strong politically. I suppose you have been here long enough to know how important The Mill is in this town. They seem to see to it that things go along the way they want. Now I have heard of several cases, and I know of some myself, where business tried to come into this town. They get just so far and then nothing happens. Any kind of new activity just can't get started in this town. There is the Johnson factory building. Several people have been interested in getting it started, but nothing ever seems to happen. The people at The Mill bought up the plant and started something there, but after a while it folded up and the building just sits there. It seems an awful waste; but The Mill group owns it so nobody else can get in there." [116]

Those who complain about Mill policies far outnumber those in favor.[117]

Several comments should be made at this point. First, Hollingshead flatly contradicts Warner's allegation that the Mill was unpopular.[118] Warner, too, indicates some uncertainty about the Mill's standing in the community, since he reports evidence both that Millworkers were underpaid and that they were adequately paid.[119]

Warner implies that the Mill was successfully depressing the economy of the town despite opposition. But Warner himself records the Mill's efforts to "start something" at the old Johnson plant. The failure of this project can hardly be attributed to the connivance of the Mill management since it would have been much cheaper to buy up the plant and *not* try to "start something" there at all. Furthermore, Warner mentions a substantial "leakage" of the Jonesville labor force to other nearby com-

115. Warner, *Jonesville*, p. 101.   116. Ibid., p. 103.
117. Ibid.   118. Hollingshead, *Elmtown*, p. 374.
119. Warner, *Jonesville*, pp. 106, 108, 112.

munities when war industries opened up job opportunities there.[120] This to be sure did less than it might have for the economy of the town, but it also suggests that hardship due to Jonesville's comparative lethargy did not necessarily fall on the lower classes.

The concern of Elmtown's politicians for Mr. Waddell's civic views is perhaps worth noting, but Warner presents no evidence to indicate that the Mill manager got his way on any burning issue. Hollingshead records one interesting situation, however; years before, Waddell apparently had led the lower classes in the successful fight for school improvements, over the objections of his fellow members of Class I.[121]

Perhaps the most important community conflict in which the Mill management engaged was the fight over unionization, which they lost. This seems to refute the thesis that the upper classes prevailed. But, curiously enough, Warner argues in effect that, win or lose, the upper classes win. This is because Warner sees unions as symptomatic of regrettable changes in American society,[122] changes which include (a) (once again) blocked job mobility within the company for workers, (b) a correspondingly increased dependence on "impersonal" union and company bureaucracies for decision-making affecting their daily lives, and (c) an increase in class conflict. There is no doubt some truth in these observations, particularly insofar as they call attention to increases in the dependence of people in local communities on superlocal institutions. However, Warner fails to give consideration to the possibility that unionization benefited workers and the community by channeling, directing, and even muting class conflict, by providing new incentives for successful community participation by members of the lower classes, and by supplying new sources of social status and social affiliation and new bases of local political power.[123]

In the present context, it is important to note that unionization becomes, through Warner's ingenious interpretation, not a sign of increasing

120. Ibid., pp. 266–68.   121. Hollingshead, *Elmtown*, p. 135.
122. Cf. also Warner's comments in YC 4.
123. For instances where unions have performed these functions see C. W. M. Hart, "Industrial Relations Research and Social Theory," *Canadian Journal of Economics and Political Science*, 15 (Feb. 1949), 53–73; Charles R. Walker, *Steeltown* (New York, Harper, 1950); Nelson N. Foote, "The Professionalization of Labor in Detroit," *Am. J. Soc.*, 58 (Jan. 1953), 371–80; George H. Hildebrand, "American Unionism, Social Stratification, and Power," *Am. J. Soc.*, 58 (Jan. 1953), 381–90; Robert E. Lane, *Political Life* (Glencoe, Free Press, 1959), p. 322; James B. McKee, "Status and Power in the Industrial Community: A Comment on Drucker's Thesis," *Am. J. Soc.*, 58 (Jan. 1953), 362–70. See also Seymour Martin Lipset, *Political Man* (Garden City, Doubleday, 1960), pp. 21–96.

power among lower status groups, but the opposite. Warner sees unions as imposing new hardships on workers without ameliorating their subordination to higher status groups. The breakup of community social patterns—especially status mobility patterns—is heralded by unionization, but corresponding benefits are left unmentioned.

It is not easy from the evidence about Morris given in these two studies to test the empirical propositions on power proposed by the stratification theory. The workers did unionize, but relatively little was done about the schools. Control of the political parties seems to have been quite decentralized. Aside from the composition of the school board, city and county government are not discussed. The bases of community power which can be inferred from the discussions in both books include (1) high status (e.g. membership in Rotary), (2) high economic position (e.g. managership in the Mill), (3) political office (e.g. in the case of the influential Republican judge), (4) access to organs of publicity (e.g. in the case of the politically important newspaper editor), (5) outside political connections (e.g. in the cases of the politically influential Republican lawyer and local Democrats who received patronage from the state organization), and (6) solidarity and numbers (e.g. in the case of the successfully unionized workers).

Aside from statements that civic leaders consulted with Waddell, the Mill manager, and acted as "agents of Class I interests," there is nothing in the two books to support the contention that civic leaders were in fact subordinate to high status persons. Indeed, in the school crisis the Board of Education seems not to have been subservient to the demands of Class I. This indicates that the composition of the power elite was not what Warner and Hollingshead say it was. In addition the diversity of bases from which members of the community could apparently exercise power seems to show that no single elite group ruled Morris.

Hollingshead and Warner are quite firm, however, in asserting that many community decisions were "rigged" in favor of the upper classes. The examples given from interviews and recounted from community folklore seem vivid enough. Yet it would be a mistake to infer from this that all community decisions followed this pattern. The assignment of "gains" and "losses" to segments of the community is at best arbitrary and difficult.

Consider the question: who gained and who lost as the result of the run-down condition of the local high school? One answer might be that, as a result of prevailing policies, high school facilities tended to be in scarce supply and lower-class children were squeezed out. But another reply, diametrically opposed, would hold that lower-class children would tend to drop out anyway, and that the real loss was sustained by the children of the upper classes, because Hollingshead's figures indicate that much higher percentages of children from these classes attended school and hence were forced to put up with an inadequate school system.[124]

A similar problem is involved when we consider the effect of the drain on Morris' working force by an out-of-town war-boom industry. These workers were forced to travel a long way to the job but were rewarded with unprecedentedly high wages, which they may or may not have spent with Morris merchants. The existence of competition for labor may or may not have forced Morris industries to raise their own pay scales, and may or may not have caused a certain number of workers to be permanently removed from the Morris labor force by out-migration. Assuming that a power elite did exist, what decisions could it have made in this real life situation to maximize its own advantage while minimizing that of others?

There are, finally, some indications that the ambiguity of class positions on a variety of issues was reflected in intraclass cleavages, as in the school controversy, and in mutually advantageous alliances between segments of several classes, as in the political party organizations.

From the data provided us about Morris, then, it is possible to construct a plausible argument which effectively denies each empirical proposition of stratification power theory.

PHILADELPHIA

Digby Baltzell's book, *Philadelphia Gentlemen*, is perhaps unique among full-scale stratification studies. One theme Baltzell promises to explore is the question, "What is the pattern of upper class control in the city?,"[125] yet he discusses this point without recourse to a single fact save the observation that businessmen predominate in the Philadelphia *Social Register*. This *tour de force* is accomplished by means of the judicious use of statements which are either proposals about the use of language (definitions) or are otherwise devoid of empirical reference. For example, Baltzell says: "An upper class may or may not be a ruling class . . . However, if it is not a ruling class, it will soon be replaced by a new upper class."[126]

The upper class, in Baltzell's terminology, refers to a group of families

124. Hollingshead, *Elmtown,* pp. 330–35.
125. Baltzell, *Philadelphia,* p. 32.   126. Ibid., p. 34.

of highest status and old wealth. "In the last analysis," Baltzell says, "power over other people is the indispensable mark of high social status, and the primary function of an upper class is the exercise of power." [127]

It seems reasonable to infer from the above that Baltzell is suggesting that high status and wealth in combination are necessary but not sufficient conditions for the exercise of power in Philadelphia. The sufficient condition, it appears, is performance of the community's "goal-integrating function," which Baltzell defines as the province of Philadelphia's business elite.[128] The men of this business elite "perform essentially similar elite functions: the exercise of power over other men in making the decisions which shape the ends of a predominantly business-oriented social structure." [129]

Baltzell provides two indications of the subordination of Philadelphia's politicians to the upper class. First, he notes that the community's aristocracy historically has had no "itch for public office." [130] Philadelphia's is a moneyed, not a public-spirited aristocracy. In any event, public office is not envisaged as a necessary condition of power because the political and opinion-making elite, according to Baltzell, "serve the ends of the business elite." [131]

It is apparently also the case in Philadelphia that a single group exercised considerable power over a wide range of activities. "Of course," Baltzell says, "economic and political power are indivisible aspects of social power." [132]

Exactly 42 Philadelphians in 1940 were, in Baltzell's judgment, in a position to exercise this power. These 42 men were listed in *Who's Who*— Baltzell's operational definition for elite membership—and were also members of either the Philadelphia or the Rittenhouse Club. They "can be said to constitute a primary group of power and influence at the top of the social structure." [133] The decisions made by these Philadelphia gentlemen, judging from their directorships, ranged from the affairs of the city's banks and financial institutions, including the Pennsylvania Railroad, to the University of Pennsylvania and the Symphony Orchestra.[134]

But the empirical basis on which these assertions rest is slim indeed. This can perhaps best be seen by recapitulating in brief and orderly form the argument in which Baltzell describes the "pattern of upper class control."

127. Ibid., p. 60.
128. Ibid., pp. 34–35.
129. Ibid., p. 35.
130. Ibid., e.g., pp. 170, 364.
131. Ibid., p. 35.
132. Ibid., p. 364.
133. Ibid., p. 365.
134. Ibid., pp. 366–71.

1.1   The Ruling Class performs society's goal-integrating functions (given by definition).

1.2   Society's goal-integrating functions are performed by business-men (given by definition).

1.3   Hence: The Ruling Class consists of businessmen.

2.1   The Upper Class is that group appearing in the *Social Register* (given by definition).

2.2   Most Philadelphians appearing in the *Social Register* are busi-ness and financial leaders (an empirical observation).

2.3   Hence: The Upper Class = The Ruling Class.[135]

Baltzell's assertions that businessmen ruled are entirely without founda-tion in his data, which consists of information from the Philadelphia *Social Register*, *Who's Who in America*, *The Dictionary of American Biography*, and a large number of biographical essays, reminiscences, and memoirs. While these sources are many, they are not diverse. They pro-vide an excellent—if somewhat accidental—report of the status aspira-tions and rituals of certain socially-minded Philadelphians, but nothing on *power*. No community issues are discussed within the pages of Balt-zell's book. No collective decisions are reached, no conflicts over com-munity resources take place, no activities of actors seeking values are described.[136] It is therefore surprising that Baltzell should conclude: "In the last analysis, power over other people is the indispensable mark of high social status, and the primary function of an upper class is the exercise of power." [137] *Philadelphia Gentlemen* is a stratification study which makes assertions about community power, but does not test them.

135. Ibid., pp. 34 ff.
136. See, in contrast, James Reichley, *The Art of Government: Reform and Or-ganization Politics in Philadelphia* (New York, Fund for the Republic, 1959).
137. Baltzell, *Philadelphia*, p. 60.

3. Research Consequences
of Stratification Theory (II)

REGIONAL CITY (ATLANTA, GEORGIA)

Just as the Middletown books mark both the beginning and the high point of an earlier era in the study of community power, the work of Floyd Hunter dominates the contemporary scene. Hunter is the author or co-author of three books dealing with what he calls "power structure." [1] All have been favorably reviewed, and the first, a study of power in a southern metropolis, Regional City, has had many imitators as well as admirers in the few years since its publication.[2]

As Hunter describes Regional City, it was run by a small group of powerful men who interacted socially and determined policy informally and behind the scenes. "The test for admission to this circle of decision-

1. Hunter, CPS; Floyd Hunter, Ruth Connor Schaffer, and Cecil B. Sheps, *Community Organization: Action and Inaction* (Chapel Hill, Univ. of North Carolina Press, 1956); Hunter, *Top Leadership, U.S.A.* (Chapel Hill, Univ. of North Carolina Press, 1959).

2. Hunter's method for studying community power, or variants thereof, can be found in Robert E. Agger, "Power Attributions in the Local Community," *Social Forces*, 34 (May 1956), 322–31; Agger and Vincent Ostrom, "The Political Structure of a Small Community," *Public Opinion Quarterly*, 20 (Spring 1956), 81–89; Agger and Ostrom, "Political Participation in a Small Community," in Heinz Eulau et al., eds., *Political Behavior* (Glencoe, Free Press, 1957), pp. 138–48; Agger and Daniel Goldrich, "Community Power Structures and Partisanship," *Am. Soc. Rev.*, 23 (August 1958), 383–92; Ernest A. T. Barth and Baha Abu-Laban, "Power Structure and the Negro Sub-community," *Am. Soc. Rev.*, 24 (Feb. 1959), 69–76; George M. Belknap and Ralph Smuckler, "Political Power Relations in a Mid-west City," *Public Opinion Quarterly*, 20 (Spring 1956), 73–81; Miller, "Industry and CPS," 9–15; Miller, "Decision-making Cliques in Community Power Structures," *Am. J. Soc.*, 64 (Nov. 1958), 299–310; Robert O. Schulze and Leonard U. Blumberg, "The Determination of Local Power Elites," *Am. J. Soc.*, 63 (Nov. 1957), 290–96; Edwin Hoffman Rhyne, "Political Parties and Decision-making in Three Southern Counties," *Am. Pol. Sci. Rev.*, 52 (Dec. 1958), 1091–1107. This method is praised highly in many places, including Gordon Blackwell, "Community Analysis," in Roland Young, ed., *Approaches to the Study of Politics* (Evanston, Northwestern Univ. Press, 1958), pp. 305–17; William J. Gore and Fred S. Silander, "A Bibliographical Essay on Decision-making," *Administrative Science Quarterly*, 4 (June 1959), 106–21.

makers," Hunter says, "is almost wholly a man's position in the business community in Regional City." [3]

The accompanying subordination of civic leaders and politicians to this power elite took many forms. Hunter outlines a division of labor in which the topmost leaders, comprising men with important economic connections, made basic policy decisions. "The men in the under-structure of power become the doers and are activated by the policy-makers—the initiators." [4]

> Most association presidents, however, remain in the under-structure of the power hierarchy. The organizations are not a sure route to sustained community prominence. Membership in the top brackets of one of the stable economic bureaucracies is the surest road to power, and this road is entered into by only a few. Organizational leaders are prone to get the publicity; the upper echelon economic leaders the power. [5]

Hunter speaks of Regional City's two most important politicians in these words: "Their interest may be said to be primarily business in the strict sense of the word. Both have a popular following that has kept them in office, but their close associates are businessmen." [6]

Hunter tells us that even the governor of the state was controlled by economic interests; "As the investigation proceeded, it became apparent that an economic elite member was the power behind the Governor." [7] In fact, Hunter says, on a matter of importance to Regional City the governor would seek out this businessman, who "had the responsibility for contacts with the Governor" though he himself was "subordinate to at least two other men of financial power in the community." [8]

What kind of policy resulted from this close control by Regional City's businessmen? Hunter says: "When new policy is laid down it must be consistent with the general scheme of old policy and should not radically change basic alignments of settled policy . . . so that the basic equilibrium in the social systems of the community may undergo as little disruption as possible." [9] "Any individual who comes to know the inner workings of many organizations reputedly devoted to the discussion of civic and social issues knows they are actually operated in the interests of the political and economic status quo." [10]

3. Hunter, *CPS*, p. 79.
5. Ibid., pp. 86–87.
7. Ibid., p. 175.
9. Ibid., p. 209.
4. Ibid., p. 100.
6. Ibid., p. 81.
8. Ibid., pp. 162–63.
10. Ibid., p. 258.

Those who are disadvantaged by the present arrangements are not an articulate group: and, while some of the professionals [Hunter apparently here refers to social service professionals] may speak for a portion of this group, they often do so only with halfhearted conviction. . . . When some of the professional and other under-structure personnel speak in behalf of the underprivileged groups they may be making an ill-defined bid for "political" support of the latter and are setting forth a veiled demand for inclusion in policy determination among the power leaders. Such disguised and scarcely conscious demands are recognized by the top leaders for what they are—a restiveness in the under-structure personnel—and they are handled accordingly. The method of handling the relatively powerless understructure is through the pressures previously described—warning, intimidations, threats and in extreme cases violence. In some cases the method may include isolation from all sources of support for the individual, including his job and therefore his income. The principle of "divide and rule" is as applicable in the community as it is in larger units of political patterning, and it is as effective.[11]

The methods Hunter used in reaching these conclusions have gained widespread acceptance as an economical, systematic, quantitative, and scientifically appropriate approach to the study of community power. It seems important, then, to undertake a critical reconstruction of this approach before considering his conclusions.

Hunter's first step was to procure four lists of leaders from the managers of civic organizations. The community council provided a list of leaders in community affairs; the chamber of commerce supplied lists of business and financial leaders; "The League of Women Voters provided lists of local political leaders who had at least major governmental committee chairmanship status"; and "newspaper editors and other civic leaders provided lists of society leaders and leaders of wealth." [12]

Hunter then asked a panel of 14 judges to cut these lists, totaling "more than 175" names, by giving "their opinions on who were the top leaders on each of the lists." All 14 judges "revealed a high degree of correlation in their choices." Hunter ended up with a roster of 40 names representing the 10 highest scoring nominees from each list.[13] This presumably means that the final 40 consists of 10 community leaders, 10 business and financial leaders, 10 local political leaders, and 10 leaders of society and wealth.

11. Ibid., pp. 247–48.   12. Ibid., p. 269.
13. Ibid., pp. 61, 269.

Hunter provides a chart of the occupational positions of these 40 top leaders which reveals quite a different picture, however. Twenty-eight are classified as in banking, commerce, finance, or the private practice of law; two as labor leaders; one as a dentist. Five are classified as "social leaders," and four as in government—two of these in the community's school system.[14]

Some of the apparent discrepancies can be explained away. First, Hunter says that his 14 judges could not agree on the "status-society" leaders. He explains: "In a sense, therefore, names given in this area of possible leadership were arbitrarily included."[15] It is possible that Hunter supplemented his list of five "social leaders" with five high-status people who were also business and financial leaders in the community. Assuming that this is what happened, and that all 10 community leaders were also business and financial leaders, we can account for 25 of the 28 individuals on the occupational list who were classified as business and financial leaders. It is still necessary to account for the other three, and also to discover what became of the six people who were apparently subtracted from the list of 10 local political leaders, since only four of these appear in the occupational listing. And where do the latter leaders and the dentist fit into the four lists of 10?

This is not so much a criticism of Hunter's panel device as of the way he used it in Regional City. A more basic objection can be raised. Consider the question Hunter asked, first of his original list-makers, then of his panel. He wanted them to name the community's top leaders, which presupposes that a group of top leaders exists.[16] In Chapter 2 (p. 29) it was pointed out that this presumption appears elsewhere in stratification writings on community power. In a study such as the one Hunter was conducting, this presupposition creates great methodological difficulties. First, how many "top leaders" are there? Second, what differentiates

14. Ibid., p. 76.   15. Ibid., p. 269.

16. This criticism of Hunter was first made by Herbert Kaufman and Victor Jones, "The Mystery of Power," *Public Administration Review,* 14 (Summer 1954), 205–12. Other critiques of Hunter include Robert A. Dahl, "Hierarchy, Democracy and Bargaining in Politics and Economics," in *Research Frontiers in Politics and Government* (Washington, Brookings, 1955), pp. 45–69; Dahl, "Critique," pp. 463–69; Norton E. Long, "The Local Community as an Ecology of Games," *Am. J. Soc.,* 64 (Nov. 1958), 251–61; Nelson W. Polsby, "The Sociology of Community Power: A Reassessment," *Social Forces,* 37 (March 1959), 232–36; Polsby, "Three Problems in the Analysis of Community Power," *Am. Soc. Rev.,* 24 (Dec. 1959), 796–803; Peter H. Rossi, "Community Decision-making," *Administrative Science Quarterly,* 1 (June 1957), 415–43; Raymond E. Wolfinger, "Reputation and Reality in the Study of 'Community Power,'" *Am. Soc. Rev.,* 25 (Oct. 1960), 636–44.

"top" from "nontop" leaders? Third, how do we know the judges are applying standards of "topness" consistent with one another and with Hunter? Fourth, how do we know the judges are correct, that in fact there *are* "top leaders" in the community, and that, if there are, they have been correctly identified?

The answer to the first question is that there is in principle no fixed number. Hunter depends on the agreement of his judges, which is at best a statistical artifact, to determine part of his answer to this question.[17] In part, he answers the question "arbitrarily" and in part, as we have seen in the case of the six missing politicians, answers were obtained which Hunter does not explain at all. Forty does not seem too large a number of top leaders for a community whose population approached half a million. But why not 41, or 39? Hunter begs this question, and in the process raises a host of others, by asserting that there were top leaders not on his list of 40 and that some on his list were not leaders. In a letter to me, Hunter says "certainly the 'social elite' [presumably the five classed as "social leaders"] were not *power* leaders." [18] In his text, Hunter gives examples of members of the top 40 who were sycophants, playboys, nonresidents of the community, and in other ways marginal or dependent on the business elite.[19] What, then, is this list of 40? "The men described," says Hunter, "come within the range of the center of power in the community." [20]

Only a rudimentary "power pyramid" of Regional City will be presented . . . I doubt seriously that power forms a single pyramid with any nicety in a community the size of Regional City. There are *pyramids* of power in this community which seem more important to the present discussion than a pyramid . . .[21] The men being interviewed represented at least a nucleus of power grouping . . .[22] This pattern of a relatively small decision-making group working through a larger under-structure is a reality, and if data were available, the total personnel involved in a major community project might possibly form a pyramid of power, but the constituency of the

17. See Wolfinger, "Reputation and Reality."

18. Letter of May 21, 1959.

19. See, for example, the descriptions in *CPS* of the following members of the Regional City power elite: Avery Spear (pp. 33–36), Edward Stokes (p. 35), Gloria Stevens (pp. 36–39), Herman Schmidt (pp. 39–41), and Percy Latham (pp. 41–42). The names are, of course, fictitious.

20. Ibid., p. 61.   21. Ibid., p. 62.

22. Ibid., p. 65.

pyramid would change according to the project being acted upon. In other words, the personnel of the pyramid would change depending upon what needs to be done at a particular time.[23]

But at other points Hunter says:

> The relative stability of the top policy-making group is a pattern quite apparent in Regional City civic affairs . . .[24] The top leaders, the under-structure professionals, and the Negro community leaders represent community groups. They are identifiable groups . . . definitely groups.[25]

In Regional City, then, the question of how many "top" leaders there were was largely an arbitrary matter, determined either by the agreement of a panel or, in the absence of agreement, by Hunter himself.

The criteria by which top leaders were separated from lesser leaders are impossible to reconstruct, except by inference from the fact that so many business leaders landed on the final list. If it is impossible to reconstruct the standards by which the judges made their decisions, it is doubly impossible to determine the extent to which individual judges applied these standards consistently one with another.

Now we come to the question: how do we know the panel named the men who really were the top leaders of the community? This question is much more troublesome than it appears. Suppose we instruct a panel to name all those meeting criterion A as leaders. In order to determine whether the panel is correct or not, we find out which men in the community meet criterion A. However, this makes the panel superfluous, since we would then have already discovered who the top leaders are (i.e. who met criterion A). The same holds true for any additional number of criteria we wish to introduce. But it was precisely because Hunter had no clear criteria for top leadership that he enlisted his panel in the first place, and this fact makes a check on the panel's correctness impossible. This means that a panel is either superfluous or its opinions are impossible to corroborate or disprove.[26]

The panel method can be considered from still another perspective. Presumably what is being determined when judges are asked to identify influentials is who has a *reputation* for being influential. This reputation can be divided into that part which is justified by behavior and that part which is not so justified. It is clearly those in the community whose be-

23. Ibid.　　　　　　　　　　24. Ibid., p. 93.
25. Ibid., p. 61.　　　　　　　　26. See Scoble, "Yankeetown."

havior in the main justifies their reputation as leaders whom social scientists would want to call the "real" leaders in the community. In other words, asking about reputations is asking, at a remove, about behavior. It can be argued that the researcher should make it his business to study behavior directly rather than depend on the opinions of secondhand sources.

Against this criticism, as we have seen, stratification writers claim that leadership takes place behind the scenes, where only insiders in the locality can penetrate. This brings into play recourse to an infinite regression, in which the "real" leaders are always held to be "behind" those whom firsthand evidence reveals as leaders.[27] A recent research finding by Schulze and Blumberg indicates, in addition, that expertise in identifying community leaders is by no means an esoteric gift.[28] Essentially the same "leaders-by-reputation" were picked by three panels drawn from different sources—all of them of relatively high status—in the population of "Cibola," Michigan.

There are four possible alternative defenses from advocates of the panel method against this finding. First, it can be asserted that none of the panels were sufficiently expert to judge who the "real" leaders of Cibola were. This explanation can be discarded, however, on the ground that at least one and possibly more of the panels were made up of people whose outward characteristics appear to have been roughly the same as panels for whom "genuine" expertise has been claimed in sociological studies.[29] The second counter-argument would be that each panel had access to inside information likely to be denied an enterprising researcher. This would mean that each panel withheld from the researcher the grounds for its ratings of leaders, and it presupposes the existence of

27. Dahl, "Critique."
28. "The Determination of Local Power Elites."
29. Miller, "Industry and CPS," Barth and Abu-Laban, "Power Structure," and Hunter, CPS, p. 269, do not describe their panels in very much detail, but apparently panel members in these studies were of relatively high status. In Regional City, for example, Hunter's 14 panel members were "business executives and professional people." Schulze and Blumberg's three panels consisted of (1) the heads of voluntary organizations, (2) political and civic leaders, and (3) the "economic dominants." None of the earlier criticisms of Warner's use of an essentially upper-class panel for stratifying communities by status reputation seems to have had much effect on the use of this method for studying power relations, despite very clear signs that similar weaknesses prevail. See Ruth R. Kornhauser, "The Warner Approach to Social Stratification," in R. Bendix and S. M. Lipset, eds., Class, Status and Power (Glencoe, Free Press, 1953), pp. 224–55, esp. p. 253; also S. M. Lipset and R. Bendix, "Social Status and Social Structure," British Journal of Sociology, 2 (June, Sept. 1951), 150–68, 230–54.

secrets about leadership activity widely known in the community itself. Obviously facts widely enough known to be available to all three panels can hardly be considered secret. A third possibility is that the panels were sufficiently expert but based their ratings on the common stock of information available to everybody, rather than on inside knowledge. Or, fourth, they reported firsthand observations any reasonably diligent researcher could have made.

The defenses against the Schulze and Blumberg finding are clearly unsatisfactory. Their finding therefore effectively denies the panel's special knowledge, and renders the test for expertise—assuming the unlikely possibility that one could be devised—moot.

Since Hunter chose to allow his panel of judges to play such a critical part in finding facts about power, it is important to note that he gives several indications that he either mistrusted or disregarded the findings of the panel. One example is the treatment of the status elite list, mentioned above. Another is his decision to conduct a separate analysis of Regional City's Negro subcommunity:

> The need to study the Negro subcommunity in Regional City grew out of field experience. This community was found to represent a sub-power grouping of considerable significance which could not be overlooked, particularly since many of the issues suggested to the field investigator by white power personnel revolved around Negro-white relations.[30]

We have already noted that Hunter insists that some of the top 40 named by his panel were not leaders at all.

It must be concluded that Hunter does not make a very strong case for the use of the panel in community power analysis. As we have seen, he provides no standard by which the panel's work can be judged and no reliable guidelines which his panel can follow in its work. He gives no defense of the special qualifications or expertise of the panel, and indeed on certain occasions replaces its judgment with his own. Finally, he gives positive indications that he disbelieves or mistrusts many of the panel's findings.

We move now to the third step in his method, which entailed interviewing 27 of the 40 top leaders. These 27 were asked many questions, among them: (1) Have any top leaders been left off the list of 40? (2) How many men would need to be involved in a major community project

30. Hunter, *CPS*, p. 270.

in Regional City to put it over? (3) If a project were before the community that required *decision* by a group of leaders—leaders that nearly everyone would accept—which 10 on the list of 40 would you choose? (4) Who is the biggest man in town? [31]

The answers reveal a great deal about Hunter's method. First, Hunter reports that some 64 people not on his list were spontaneously nominated as top leaders. One man was named five times and five men were nominated four times. Hunter never changed his list of top leaders to include these nominees, however.[32]

No coherent pattern of responses seem to have been received to the second question. "The answers to this question," Hunter reports, "varied from: 'you've got the men right here on this list—maybe ten of them,' to 'fifty to a hundred.'" [33] In response to the third question, one man, George Delbert, received the most mentions but, in question four, the "biggest man in town" was discovered to be someone entirely different, Charles Homer.[34] The first observation that should be made is that, insofar as the identification of leaders is concerned, Hunter's interviewing contributed only a little new information, and most of it tended to discredit the notion that there was a homogeneous, discrete, top leadership group in Regional City.

Hunter develops other evidence in the course of the interviews which casts doubt on the propositions of the stratification theory. For example, he reports that the lowest economic and status group in Regional City, the Negroes, were by virtue of their political solidarity very powerful in community affairs.

> Within the city limits of Regional City almost a third of the population are Negroes. Thousands of them are registered voters, and on issues which affect them directly they are prone to follow the Organized Voters' lead in their choice of candidates. Cries of "pocket voting" are always raised by the unfavored candidate, but this only tends to weld the Negro vote into a more solid expression of political strength. Everyone politically inclined is aware of the power of the Negro vote to swing elections within the city, and Smith [a Negro political leader] gets unfeigned deference from the city's elected officials, as well as from many of the state politicians.[35]

31. Ibid., pp. 61 ff., 268–71. Emphasis Hunter's.
32. Ibid., pp. 64–65.
33. Ibid., p. 65.
34. Ibid., pp. 62, 64.
35. Ibid., p. 50.

In spite of the alleged subordination of politicians to the power elite, Hunter describes the following situation:

> After the policy line had been set and before the project could be activated, it was necessary to go to the state legislature for enabling legislation. In this process the legislators bargained with the [upper-class] policy group concerning the membership of the proposed official committee. During the horse-trading, some of the names proposed by the policy-makers were dropped in favor of local politicos agreeable to the state leaders.[36]

Contrary to the third key proposition of stratification theory, it is exceedingly important to specify issues in discussing power in Regional City. In the course of his interviews with what turned out to be an unexplained preponderance of community businessmen, Hunter asked how they went about influencing concrete policy decisions. The issues Hunter ended up treating at greatest length in his book included (1) getting an international trade association to locate in Regional City, (2) the fate of the Progressive party in Old State, (3) the decision of members of the power elite to testify in Washington before Congress on a pending tax bill, (4) getting a new industry in Regional City, (5) the political views of a columnist in a community trade publication.[37] All of these issues were either trivial or clearly of predominant concern to businessmen, or both. Furthermore, they seem to have been issues on which Hunter's "power elite" met with relative success, in contrast to other issues Hunter lists, of much wider concern in the community, where the "power elite" was either split wide open or united but ineffective. These issues included: (1) the plan of development, (2) the sales tax, (3) traffic control, and (4) race relations. In further contradiction of the notion that there is a single power elite, it is obvious that many other actors were involved in decision-making on these issues, although Hunter tells us nothing of their goals and activities.[38]

One informant, James Treat, explained the system of policy-formation in the Regional City business community as a process of negotiation among at least five independent "crowds" of leaders. These crowds sometimes competed and sometimes entered into alliances with one another on specific community programs.[39]

This description of occasional social conflict among elite groups does not exclude the possibility of interclass rivalry, of course. Hunter de-

36. Ibid., p. 98.   37. Ibid., pp. 160, 164 ff., 175 ff.
38. Ibid., pp. 207–27.   39. Ibid., pp. 75 ff.

scribes the position of the lower strata as hierarchically subordinate rather than opposed to the power elite. He sees the "under-structure," as he calls it, as primarily involved in executing policies set by the power elite. He does not view these policies as always detrimental to the lower classes. Hunter intimates that dire things *would* happen to the lower classes if they stepped out of line, but only the case of the trade paper columnist is offered in point.[40] On the other hand, members of the lower-class Negro minority apparently exercised a considerable influence over many community policies.

It is most extraordinary to observe that Hunter limits the role of the alleged decision-makers to the relatively innocuous task of "getting consent." He specifically denies that the top members of the pyramid had special opportunities either to *innovate* or to *execute* policies. It has already been noted that one of Hunter's major points is that the "top leaders" of Regional City rarely appeared as leaders of community organizations or as executors of community policy.[41] This indicates, says Hunter, that the top leadership "delegated" the detail work downward after basic policies were set. One would expect, then, that the effectiveness of the power elite rested on its ability to initiate action and to innovate in community policy. But in this area of activity, Hunter reports, "The power leaders have action initiated for them more often than they initiate action." [42] "Of all the men talked to in Regional City, only one [the Mayor] indicated that he was aggressive in 'raising issues' for a realignment of policy." [43]

Apparently members of the power elite felt greatly constrained with respect to their ability to operate in the community. Hunter says, "a careful watch is kept for what 'will go' and what 'will not go.' " [44] This may be taken as an indication of lack of conflict among the classes and of the importance that Regional City decision-makers placed upon a widespread distribution of benefits.

How have the five key propositions of stratification theory fared in our re-examination of Hunter's discussion of Regional City? We cannot, on the evidence, conclude that the upper class ruled, that political and civic leaders were subordinate to them, that there was a power elite, that the interests of a single class were served by community policies, or that social conflicts sharply divided the classes. While Hunter claims that every one of these propositions held true in Regional City, his methods for

40. Ibid., pp. 247–48.
42. Ibid., p. 226.
44. Ibid., p. 111.

41. Ibid., passim, esp. pp. 92 ff.
43. Ibid., p. 209.

collecting the facts on these points are suspect, and much unexplained contrary evidence appears in his book. Hunter does not present enough evidence to justify an attempt at formulating an alternative description of power in Regional City, but there is more than enough to cast doubt on his own description.

BIGTOWN (BATON ROUGE, LOUISIANA)

While an over-representation of businessmen in the interview sample may be regarded as an unhappy accident in Hunter's case, Roland Pellegrin and Charles Coates develop their discussion of power in Bigtown from an apparently purposely restricted group of "intensive interviews with 50 leading executives of the community and other persons who have worked with and observed corporation executives." [45]

In spite of the limitations within which they operated in collecting data, Pellegrin and Coates turn up a good many contradictions of stratification theory, which they analyze in an especially ingenious manner. They begin by asserting:

> The stratification system of a given community attains stability and remains basically unaltered over relatively long periods of time because . . . the control of community affairs and policies resides in dominant interest groups which feel little incentive to disrupt the existing pattern of superordination and subordination. These groups exercise power which is infinitely out of proportion to their number. [46]

But, in a footnote, Pellegrin and Coates admit that politicians were not especially cooperative with the allegedly "dominant [economic] interest groups" nor were they subservient to them.

> The typical interviewee in this study described local governmental officials as relatively powerless figures who do not have the backing of influential groups but secured their positions through the support of working-class voters. Indeed, these officials were more often than not targets of ridicule for those who evaluated their positions in the power structure.

But,

> The relative lack of integration of Bigtown's interest groups makes it possible for governmental officials to sponsor civic projects which

45. Roland J. Pellegrin and Charles H. Coates, "Absentee-owned Corporations and Community Power Structure," *Am. J. Soc., 61* (March 1956), 413–19.
46. Ibid., 413.

are sometimes successful, in spite of opposition from one or another of the "crowds" [of economic leaders]. Interest groups find it difficult to express publicly opposition to projects which attract widespread public support. To do so would be "bad public relations," perhaps unprofitable in the long run.[47]

Once again, then, the vote is mentioned as an important base of community power. Social conflict is described as occurring between competing interest groups, not classes. Pellegrin and Coates also assert that "as in Regional City, community projects can be carried out successfully only if the small group of policy-makers can marshal the cooperation of large numbers of lower-level workers who will perform the labor required to transform the policies and decisions into reality."[48]

On the other hand, Pellegrin and Coates devote most of their attention to the tactics and ideology of businessmen in community life. Their interviews turned up numerous instances in which a big-business official was expected to represent his company on citizens' committees, in part because of "an almost incredible preoccupation with 'public relations'" by the corporation and in part to "protect and foster its own interest and to promote a conservative, business-class ideology."

Executives are constantly on guard lest fellow committee members divert funds to new projects suggestive of the "welfare state." Advocates of such measures are speedily labeled "controversial" and, if they persist, are referred to as "cranks" or "subversives"—a term once used only for political traitors. Deviants of this nature are, in the long run, however, weeded out; they are not able to obtain appointments to other committees. An old-timer, involved in such measures scores of times during the previous thirty years, observed:

"We freeze out these New Dealers and other Reds. When we appoint people to important committee posts, we look at their record. If an individual has gone all out on some crazy idea, his goose is cooked. If I am chairman of a group that is making appointments, I go stone deaf whenever someone suggests the name of one of these radicals. My hearing improves when a good, reliable person is mentioned as a possibility."[49]

Despite their preoccupation with the tactics and ideology of businessmen, Pellegrin and Coates give evidence that economic leaders were

47. Ibid., 414.
48. Ibid., 418.
49. Ibid., 417.

aware that they were not as powerful as the quotations above might indicate.

> They dwell at great length upon the power structure of other cities in which they have resided, where an informal "Committee of 50," "Citizens' Council," or like group controls civic affairs with a firm hand. These glowing accounts are typically accompanied by a pessimistic description of the situation in Bigtown. This community, as analyzed by some of its outstanding men, has a number of powerful interest groups but lacks effective liaison among them and leadership to unite them. Under these circumstances, a given "crowd" is unlikely to participate in a proposed project unless it foresees tangible gain.[50]

Pellegrin and Coates reconcile evidence of fragmented policy-making with stratification theory in an original manner. While they assert that the managers of the large corporations did not constitute a dominant interest group in Bigtown, because (1) they were seldom united on community issues; (2) other groups, notably politicians with mass-based support, were more effectively mobilized; (3) executives were preoccupied with their own careers, which gave them a more cosmopolitan frame of reference; and (4) the policies of the large corporations were obsessively concerned with public relations, Pellegrin and Coates do insist that:

> Corporation support probably assures the success of a proposed project, while disapproval spells doom for it. Thus absentee-owned corporations are a decisive force in the power structure of Bigtown, since they constitute a balance of power among the competing interest groups of the community.[51]

This "decisive force" could operate only (1) when other groups in the community were about equally distributed for and against a proposal, (2) when the big-corporation executives were all more or less united on the question, and (3) when they did something about it. No doubt all three of these conditions have been met on occasion. But similar conditions can operate so as to make many groups in the community important in the "balance of power." In fact, there may have been groups in the community much more united and more effectively mobilized than businessmen, and, consequently, these groups may have tipped the "balance" much more often. By interviewing only businessmen, Pellegrin and Coates

50. Ibid., 414.   51. Ibid.

entirely ignored this possibility. Since Pellegrin and Coates contradict themselves in almost every paragraph on the five key propositions of the stratification theory, it is impossible to judge from their presentation who ruled in Bigtown.

CIBOLA (YPSILANTI, MICHIGAN)

In Robert O. Schulze's study of Cibola, a midwestern "satellite" community, the major finding was that economic domination of the community had shifted from long-time local residents and local industry into the hands of local managers of large, bureaucratized, absentee-owned corporations. A concomitant of this historical trend was the tendency for economic dominants to play a smaller and smaller part in community decision-making. This finding demonstrates that something other than economic dominance (Schulze does not make entirely clear what) had come to be important as a base of community power in Cibola.

Schulze does not elaborate on this point, however. He refers to the power structure as "bifurcated," that is, as shared between the economic dominants who monopolized "potential for determinative action," and a new power elite—"a group of middle-class business and professional men" whom he calls "public leaders"—who monopolized the "*overt* direction of the political and civic life of Cibola." [52]

Schulze is using here a combination of explanatory devices already discussed: in particular, the covertness argument, with its possibility of infinite regress in case of a direct challenge, and the and-also fallacy, which recognizes direct disproof of a proposition not by modifying or discarding the proposition but by pleading "special circumstances." As we shall see shortly, even the "public leaders" of Cibola are reported by Schulze to have been far from a united, omnipotent elite group. At any rate, the economic elite did not rule Cibola.

Schulze reports that community decisions were not especially important to present-day economic dominants for numerous reasons: because the executives themselves were geographically mobile within the company bureaucracy and had no long-term attachments to the community; because most large companies had an explicit hands-off policy vis-à-vis the community, for the sake of good public relations; and, finally, because no decisions made in Cibola seemed likely materially to affect a mam-

---

52. Emphasis supplied. This discussion is drawn from two sources: Robert O. Schulze, "The Role of Economic Dominants in Community Power Structure," *Am. Soc. Rev.*, 23 (Feb. 1958), 3–9; and Schulze, "Bifurcation." The quotations are from "The Role of Economic Dominants," 6, 8, 9.

moth, worldwide business, one of whose units was located there. However, Schulze believes that these large corporations *could* have determined policy had they wanted to, both in Cibola and in the larger arenas more salient to them.[53]

The assertion that any group "potentially" could exercise significant, or decisive, or any influence in community affairs is not easy to discuss in a scientific manner. How can one tell, after all, whether or not an actor is powerful unless some sequence of events, competently observed, attests to his power? If these events take place, then the power of the actor is not "potential" but actual. If these events do not occur, then what grounds have we to suppose that the actor is powerful? There appear to be no scientific grounds for such a supposition; therefore, by assigning a high "power potential" to economic dominants, and referring to this potential as one-half of a bifurcated system, Schulze is indulging in empirically unjustified speculation.

Another of Schulze's major points is that, in Cibola, the "potential" of the large companies would probably never be put to the test. He mentions two factors operating in contradictory directions with respect to the possible exploitation of the power potential of absentee-owned corporations. The first was a pronounced sensitivity on the part of many Cibola decision-makers to *any* sentiments expressed by minions of the large corporations.[54] Schulze pictures the leaders of Cibola's civic life as extremely eager to anticipate the reactions of the economic dominants; this, he believes, acted as an important constraint on community policy-making. The economic dominants reacted to the jumpiness of the city fathers by withdrawing even further from community participation, to the extent that they felt inhibited from expressing even idle or personal opinions for fear of causing inappropriately servile responses.[55]

The second, contradictory, factor was that with the economic dominants largely silent and apathetic on community issues, their roles and images in the community became subject to possible manipulation by noneconomic dominants who wished to use the large corporations' power potential to further their own ends.[56] This reverses the usual formula, which has the economic leaders doing the manipulating. Schulze does not say, incidentally, that economic dominants *were* so victimized; only that their position made them increasingly vulnerable to this kind of control by civic leaders.

53. Schulze, "Bifurcation," 49, 68–72.   54. Ibid., 68–71.
55. Ibid., and 58–60.
56. Schulze, "The Role of Economic Dominants," 8.

One lone instance was recorded by Schulze in which an economic dominant attempted to "cash in" on his "potential." The dominant in question ran for a seat on the board of directors of the Cibola Chamber of Commerce and was badly beaten.[57] With respect to larger arenas, the decay in recent years of the influence of economically dominant corporations in the politics of Michigan, where Cibola is located, is a well-known phenomenon which Schulze neither mentions nor studies.[58]

Schulze finds that economic dominants played essentially unimportant roles in Cibola's civic life. This hardly constitutes a significant contribution to an understanding of how decision-making processes in Cibola *did* work. Another aspect of Schulze's research is more clearly to the point. He reconstructs from interviews and documentary sources the circumstances and events of two community controversies. These case studies provide better information about the distribution of influence among the people Schulze identifies as "public leaders," as well as among other members of the community.

Both of these case studies involve attempts at planned community change. The attempt to institute a city manager form of government, by changing the city charter, failed at first but succeeded later, after proponents of the change made concessions to "hold-out" groups.[59] The attempt by the city to annex land in Pottawatomie township failed because, as one public leader said,

> Our real problem was that we had nothing to offer the people who carried weight in the township. The officials there are an entrenched bunch, and they know perfectly well that for every acre of land they might let us have, they'd lose money on the state sales tax diversions.[60]

Of the two case studies, the annexation battle is the less informative because it involves negotiations between a relatively united set of community leaders on the one hand and an intransigent group of politicians outside the community on the other.

The charter battle, which was carried on entirely within the community, is more relevant. Schulze points out that the major difference between the first round of the charter fight, which proponents of

57. Ibid., 4; "Bifurcation," 20, 48–49.

58. See Duncan Norton-Taylor, "What's Wrong with Michigan?" *Fortune* (Dec. 1955), 142 ff. The election by a narrow margin of a Republican businessman to the governorship of the state in 1962 after a 16-year famine does not materially alter the force of this point, I think.

59. Schulze, "Bifurcation," 60.   60. Ibid., 63.

change lost, and the second round, which they won, was a broadening
of the base of decision-making, to include, for example, "younger business and professional men in the community." [61]

> Likewise [Schulze says], the public leaders, following the charter's
> defeat in March, had been obliged to try to "win over" certain key
> leaders in the Negro and working class sub-communities.[62]

> The second charter vote indicated that they succeeded in these
> efforts. But in the process, promises and commitments had been
> made—as evidenced by the fact that since 1946 one prominent
> Negro leader and one pivotal labor union official almost invariably
> have been named to "represent" their elements in the community
> on important citizen committees appointed by the Chamber of
> Commerce and the city council. In all of these instances, a some-
> what wider sharing in the decision-making processes resulted.[63]

Others to whom concessions had to be made were the professional
politicians—themselves public leaders—who were put out of work
as a result of the adoption of the new charter. As Schulze points out:

> The men intimately involved in the informal leadership structure
> of a small community could afford neither to flaunt nor to be
> vindictive—for they realized that if the effort to renovate the local
> government was to result in the lasting alienation of significant seg-
> ments of community opinion, theirs would have been a Pyrrhic
> victory indeed.[64]

The charter episode divided the city along the lines of political interests, which coincided only adventitiously with economic and status
groupings. The economic dominants gave token approval to the charter
change. When leadership was concentrated in the hands of many of
Schulze's "public leaders," it was unsuccessful. Later, a coalition of
"public leaders" and "sub-community" leaders was successful despite
the opposition of some public leaders, namely the professional politicians.

61. Ibid., 59.

62. Ibid., 60. Schulze's use of the category "sub-community" (in which he follows
Hunter) has interesting methodological consequences. We could say, for example,
that a Negro powerful in community decision-making is a community leader. Instead,
Schulze classifies this leader according to the limits of his presumed power base and
calls him a "leader of the Negro sub-community." Only businessmen fail to receive
this treatment, thus preserving an illusion of general pervasiveness about the influence
and activities of the leaders of the business subcommunity, which may not accord
at all with the facts.

63. Schulze "Bifurcation," 60.   64. Ibid.

There was concerted effort, as we have seen, to distribute values broadly among Cibola's economic and status groups. Indeed, Schulze indicates that this was the price of success.

To summarize: the only concrete community decision discussed at any length by Schulze calls into question all of the propositions of the stratification analysis. Whether or not the coalition that won on the charter issue held together on a variety of other issues is a question that can be answered only by examining other issues. Certainly we would not want to call the broad alliance that prevailed in the charter battle a "power elite" in the usual sense of the term, according to which the ruling or prevailing group must constitute less than a majority of the population and should also not be an artifact of the application of majoritarian principles (as in the case of a representative assembly).[65] Since the new charter was adopted in a referendum, after the leaders of a majority of the population became convinced of its desirability, it could be argued that the group that prevailed in this case was not an elite.

PACIFIC CITY (SEATTLE, WASHINGTON)

In Pacific City, an attempt was made to copy and improve upon Hunter's research in Regional City. Delbert C. Miller has written two articles on power in Pacific City, and Ernest Barth and Baha Abu-Laban have contributed an article on the power structure of Pacific City's Negro subcommunity.

Miller compares his Pacific City findings with data gathered in an English city. Among the hypotheses he seeks to test are the following: (1) Do business leaders predominate in the community's power structure?[66] (2) Is community power exercised through "cliques" of leaders?[67] Miller claims to have found evidence supporting an affirmative conclusion to the first question and a somewhat more limited affirmative to the second. But a close reading of his presentation reveals that the facts support the opposite conclusions equally well.

Miller's method of data collection is an elaboration of the Hunter technique criticized above. Community organizations and informants were asked to nominate leaders in nine (rather than four) sectors of community life. Ten judges were asked to rate the 312 resulting names as "most influential," "influential," and "less influential" according to the

65. See the discussion in Chapter 1 and in Dahl, "Critique."
66. Miller, "Industry and CPS," 9.
67. Miller, "Decision-making Cliques," 299.

specific criterion: "person participates actively either in supporting or initiating policy decisions which have the most effect on the community." [68]

Forty-four persons were nominated in this way as "most influential" in the community—a group Miller calls "Top Influentials." The next step was to interview half of these Top Influentials, who were asked, among other things, "If you were responsible for a major project which was before the community that required decision by a group of leaders —leaders that nearly everybody would accept—which ten on this list would you choose?" Those nominated most often in this manner by Top Influentials were designated "Key Influentials." [69] The top dozen Key Influentials were found to be mostly businessmen (67 per cent), and on the basis of this evidence Miller concludes: "Businessmen do exert a predominant influence in community decision-making in Pacific City." [70] "Key Influentials," Miller asserts, "are a significant feature of any community power structure for they are the sociometric leaders. The initiation and sanction of policy tends to be centered about them so that they may greatly influence the values which dominate in decision-making." [71]

This conclusion does not follow for several reasons. First, Miller's Key Influentials were picked from among Top Influentials for unanimous acceptability, and not because they initiated and sanctioned policies. Miller presents no evidence at all about the actual initiation and sanction of any community policy. Secondly, they were picked on the basis of a vague and hypothetical question, not on the basis of a concrete issue or a specific pattern of past behavior. This is very important because, as Dahl, Wolfinger, and I have pointed out, answers to Miller's question may mean many things, and their meanings are in any case irrelevant until concrete instances of policy formation are examined. [72] Also, by specifying particular issues it is possible to determine whether 12 is an appropriate number of Key Influentials. If 40 seemed too small in Regional City, 12 seems ridiculous in the hub of America's Northwest.

68. Miller, "Industry and CPS," 10.   69. Ibid.
70. Ibid., 13.   71. Ibid., 12.
72. See works previously cited. Alternative interpretations of responses to general questions which fail to enumerate specific issues, such as the ones Miller and Hunter asked, might be: Respondents (1) are naming the status elite; (2) have in mind some specific issue or issues which are (A) of recent interest, (B) especially salient to the respondent, or (C) characteristic of the community—as public power might be in the West or the race issue in the South; (3) are naming the community's old civic warhorses or primarily letterhead names; (4) are naming the community's formal leadership; (5) are naming the most vocal leaders in the community.

If these 12 Key Influentials were truly influential on an appreciable number of issues in Pacific City, then it seems unlikely that they would have had any time or energy left over to run their own businesses. If their influence was in fact restricted to only one or a few issues, then Miller should have told us what these issues were.

Miller's data are even more ambiguous with respect to his second hypothesis—that "cliques" ran Pacific City. He presents figures attesting to the following:

1. Key Influentials tend to choose one another rather than outsiders as members of the "top ten."

2. Key Influentials know more Top Influentials better, on the average, than Top Influentials know Top Influentials.

3. Key Influentials serve on more committees than Top Influentials.

4. Key Influentials tend to participate in more organizations than Top Influentials.

5. There is a slightly disproportionate tendency for Key Influentials to belong to business organizations, which, Miller believes, are the most important in the community.[73]

From this compendium of indirect evidence, Miller concludes that there is reason to believe that Key Influentials form cliques of intensively interacting people. Direct testimony on this point robs the finding of almost all meaning, however. While both Top Influentials and Key Influentials believe that "crowds" exist, Miller quotes 11 interviews—fully half the number he conducted in Pacific City—which indicate that (1) there is no "top" group of leaders, but leaders are instead specialized around specific issues (which he does not study), and (2) none of the specialized "top" groups can singlehandedly execute its policies without widespread cooperation from others in the community.[74] In spite of this testimony, Miller concludes that "The stratified pyramid, with its solidary top business elite . . . is . . . a useful guide to the power potential in Pacific City." [75] And in another place: the pyramid "applies to Pacific City for a wide range of issues and projects [unspecified] but it does not apply during many political campaigns when coalitions form and often defeat the leaders who are ranked according to the stratified model." [76]

Miller's research, in short, combines to an extraordinary degree the three symptoms of scientific inadequacy advanced at the beginning of

73. Miller, "Decision-making Cliques," 301–03.
74. Ibid., 305–10.   75. Ibid., 309.
76. Ibid., 307.

the previous chapter. First, he ignores much data which tend to discredit his thesis: specific examples of social conflict mentioned in the course of his two papers (and in Barth and Abu-Laban's companion piece) consistently deny the utility of the elaborate model of power structure he postulates. Examples of this are the political campaigns and "The defeat of the right to work issue in Pacific City in 1956." [77] Secondly, Miller's methods, which include not specifying issues and developing meaningless statistical artifacts like a 12-member "Key" elite, purport to confirm hypotheses which they do not actually test. Thirdly, by recourse to the argument of "potential" power, Miller resorts to an ad hoc explanation in order to reconcile with his thesis findings that are contrary to it.

Barth and Abu-Laban engage in something similar when they find that the Negro subcommunity "has no genuine power structure" [78]— even though on the issues most salient to them Negro leaders "have been remarkably successful." [79] The reason why Negroes are said to be without power in the community is because "Their sub-community lacked large scale business and industrial organizations and, *consequently*, no *genuine* power structure had developed." [80]

The reasoning here is crystal clear. A power structure is "genuine," to these researchers, only if they discover big businessmen in it. This explains Miller's otherwise inexplicable account indicating that the City Council of Pacific City was relatively powerless by virtue of the fact that it was made up of small businessmen.[81] The failure of Pacific City to conform to the propositions of stratification theory is attributed not to the incorrectness of the propositions but to immaturities, situations of flux, or other abnormalities in the social structure of the city.

In the latter part of his second article, Miller attempts to construct a model of community power structure applicable to Pacific City.[82] He posits a pyramid-shaped model on the one hand and a concentric ring-shaped model on the other. The second model is supposed to symbolize the accessibility of centers of power to a wider range of community leaders. Pacific City, Miller suggests, lies somewhere between these two models. Unfortunately, this conclusion suggests only

77. Ibid.
78. Barth and Abu-Laban, "Power Structure," 76.
79. Ibid., 71, 76.
80. Ibid., Abstract, p. 69. Emphasis supplied.
81. Miller, "Industry and CPS," 14–15.
82. Miller, "Decision-making Cliques," 307–10.

that the key propositions of stratification theory do not apply in Pacific City; it does not offer further information on which a corrected statement about power in Pacific City could be based.

The purpose of the second and third chapters of this book has been to examine eight stratification studies of community power, all of which are generally considered to be contributions to current knowledge about community power.[83] In all we have found reasons to mistrust the findings of their authors. In concluding this examination, it might be useful to summarize the various ways in which the authors have tried to save stratification theory despite what appears to be contradictory evidence. These have included:

1. The "false consciousness" argument, which holds that when a social group violates an analyst's expectations the group is acting "irrationally."

2. The "and-also" argument, which suggests that instances in which the analyst's expectations are not met are trivial or irrelevant.

3. The "lump of power" assumption, which denies that power can be exercised by any persons or groups not defined as being at the "top" of the status or economic structure.

4. The assumption of covertness, which allows analysts to assert that somewhere "behind the scenes" things are exactly the opposite from the way they seem.

5. The "balance of power" assumption, which holds that an apparently powerless economic elite is "really" powerful because of its (undemonstrated) strategic position among community groups.

83. Recent works citing stratification studies with approval include: Ernest A. T. Barth, "Community Influence Systems: Structure and Change," Social Forces, 40 (Oct. 1961), 58–63; Orrin E. Klapp and L. Vincent Padgett, "Power Structures and Decision-making in a Mexican Border City," Am. J. Soc., 65 (Jan. 1960), 400–06; William H. Form and Warren L. Sauer, "Organized Labor's Image of Community Power Structure," Social Forces, 38 (May 1960), 332–41; Ted C. Smith, "The Structuring of Power in a Suburban Community," Pacific Sociological Review, 3 (Fall 1960), 83–88; Peter H. Rossi, "Power and Community Structure," Midwest Journal of Political Science, 4 (Nov. 1960), 390–401; Nicholas Babchuk, Ruth Marsey, and C. Wayne Gordon, "Men and Women in Community Agencies: A Note on Power and Prestige," Am. Soc. Rev., 25 (June 1960), 399–403; Harry R. Dick, "A Method for Ranking Community Influentials," Am. Soc. Rev., 25 (June 1960), 395–99; William V. D'Antonio, William H. Form, Charles P. Loomis, and Eugene C. Erickson, "Institutional and Occupational Representations in Eleven Community Influence Systems," Am. Soc. Rev., 26 (June 1961), 440–46; Howard J. Ehrlich, "The Reputational Approach to the Study of Community Power," Am. Soc. Rev., 26 (Dec. 1961), 926–27; Richard A. Schermerhorn, Society and Power (New York, Random House, 1961), pp. 87–105.

6. The "power potential" allegation, which holds that the economic (or social) elite could determine community decisions if it wanted to, and only refrains because of lack of interest in community affairs.

These six formulas explain away evidence indicating that the economic and status elites of communities are not as important as stratification theory insists. All of these explanations share at least one common element: all are impossible to confirm or disprove *in principle*. All depend for their "correctness" upon the definitions adopted by analysts rather than upon the evidence of the facts.

Three methodological errors leading to failure to test propositions empirically have been noted. First, there is the identification, by definition, of economic or status elites with power elites, as in the cases of Miller, Barth and Abu-Laban, and Baltzell. Secondly, there is the strong propensity to interview only, or primarily, businessmen, as in the cases of Hunter, Coates and Pellegrin, and Schulze. This fundamental decision of research strategy is understandable in the light of the expectations of stratification theory, but it is incomprehensible as a device for *testing* these expectations. Thirdly, there is the habit of never specifying issues. This not only short-circuits communication between researcher and respondent and makes tests of the accuracy of responses difficult, if not impossible; but, given the disproportionate number of businessmen among respondents, it also guarantees that issues salient to businessmen will receive disproportionate attention. This in turn provides an artificially produced confirmation of the hegemony of businessmen.

Finally, factual information given in these community studies by no means unambiguously supports the five key propositions of stratification theory. Thus the conclusion of this chapter must be that the stratification studies of community power all exhibit symptoms of scientific inadequacy resembling those postulated at the beginning of Chapter 2.

4. Who Rules in New Haven?

An Empirical Test
of the Stratification Theory

The two preceding chapters point to inadequacies in a good many studies of community power, but it can be argued that none of these studies was a faithful test of the key propositions of the stratification theory. It is still possible that stratification theory gives a correct description of community power and politics in America. It appears that each of the key propositions has often been phrased so as to make it extremely difficult, if not impossible, to design empirical tests for them. The purpose of this chapter is to design and make such a test, using data from a study of New Haven, Connecticut, which was collected for the most part in the years 1957 and 1958. Perhaps the simplest way to begin would be to describe briefly the New Haven research, leaving a defense of its adequacy for later.

The major purpose of the study was to explain certain events which took place in New Haven. These events related to the making and executing of public policy in several issue-areas, of which three will be discussed here in detail: urban redevelopment, public education, and political nominations. A variety of methods were used to identify the events we wanted to study. Publicly visible participants in some events in each issue-area were identified by reading the newspapers and examining public documents. Participants in and observers of each issue-area were interviewed and asked to describe the events in which they were involved, their roles, and the roles of others. For almost a year, a member of the research group observed the course of events from a position close to the Mayor and his Development Administrator; we discovered that they were clearly the most significant actors in urban redevelopment and were quite important in other issue-areas as well. The methods used to gather data were, in other words, comparable in some ways to those of the journalist, the historian, the anthropologist, and the sociologist.[1]

In what sense were public policies in these issue-areas going to be "explained"? Since the research was organized around the question "who governs?", we wanted to frame explanations that would identify participants in policy-making and describe what they did. The intention was to arrive at some understanding of normal policy-making processes in each of three issue-areas and to compare these findings with conventional theories of policy-making—which also describe who participates and how—such as a theory of the ruling elite or a theory of majoritarian democracy. My purpose here, as distinct from the more general purposes of the New Haven study, is to present a picture of the normal policy-making processes in each of the three issue-areas and then to compare this with the picture presented in stratification theory.

URBAN REDEVELOPMENT

Urban redevelopment was the first issue-area selected for study. It was an obvious choice; the redevelopment program during the years studied was by most criteria the biggest thing in New Haven.[2] Urban redevelopment had been the focus of several campaigns for re-election by the incumbent mayor, Richard C. Lee. The program had gained nationwide publicity in popular magazines.[3] The federal government had spent, allocated, or promised more redevelopment money per capita

1. The sociologist Morris Zelditch, Jr., has written a very useful essay in which he discusses various strategies of field research, "Some Methodological Problems of Field Studies," *Am. J. Soc.*, 67 (March 1962), 566–76. Zelditch enumerates three types of information: Distributions and Frequencies, Incidents and Histories, and Generally Known Roles and Statuses. The three ways of obtaining information he mentions are Participant Observation, Interviewing Informants, and Enumerations and Samples. Each of these methods was employed in the New Haven study and all three types of information were gathered and put together in a variety of ways. For a full description of the field research methods employed in the New Haven study, see Dahl, *Who Governs?*, pp. 330–43.

2. Criteria by which policies can be ranked according to their importance are enumerated in the appendix to this chapter. No doubt other criteria will occur to the ingenious reader. But there seems, in any case, to be no doubt that each of the issue-areas studied in New Haven comfortably meets any criteria of importance likely to be proposed.

The politics of the New Haven urban redevelopment program are reported on and discussed in detail in Raymond E. Wolfinger, *The Politics of Progress*, to be published by the Yale University Press. See also Dahl, *Who Governs?*, esp. chap. 10.

3. For example, Jeanne R. Lowe, "Lee of New Haven and His Political Jackpot," *Harper's Magazine* (Oct. 1957), and Joe Alex Morris, "He Is Saving a 'Dead' City," *The Saturday Evening Post* (April 19), 1958.

to New Haven than to any other city in the nation.[4] The program was an ambitious one, involving the razing of much of the central business district and a series of projects designed to transform the physical plant of a large portion of the city.

Who wanted urban redevelopment? By 1957, practically everyone in New Haven who had anything to say in public strongly favored the program. But a few years before, urban redevelopment was not especially salient as a community issue.

The change in the climate of opinion from indifference to strong support was largely the work of one man, Mayor Lee. As an alderman, Lee had had a mild interest in city planning, but this interest was not expressed at all strongly in two losing races for mayor which Lee ran in 1949 and 1951. During the latter campaign, however, Lee recalled certain experiences that persuaded him of the need for urban redevelopment as a method of alleviating the human misery which accompanied slum life.

> I went into the homes on Oak Street and they set up neighborhood meetings for me . . . three and four in one night. And I came out from one of those homes on Oak Street, and I sat on the curb and I was just as sick as a puppy. Why, the smell of this building; it had no electricity, it had no gas, it had kerosene lamps, light had never seen those corridors in generations . . . and there . . . right there was when I began to tie in all these ideas we'd been practicing in city planning for years in terms of the human benefits that a program like this could reap for a city.

By 1953 Lee was aware of the possibilities for federal aid contained in the Housing Act of 1949. He needed a positive issue with which to confront the voters after two narrow losses at the polls in campaigns in which he felt he had concentrated too much on the shortcomings of his opponent. It would, however, be inaccurate to suppose that in 1953 Lee envisioned a redevelopment program as vast as the one subsequently undertaken. Rather, the redevelopment program grew piecemeal, as Lee's popularity and his electoral margins grew. In the beginning, urban redevelopment was not simply a social experiment testing whether the city center could be saved from blight and commercial strangulation; it was also a political experiment in which Lee sought to discover whether sufficient political support could be rallied behind such a program.

4. See Dahl, *Who Governs?*, pp. 121–33, esp. Fig. 10.1.

Lee pledged in 1953 to mount a coordinated attack on the problem of urban blight. He promised that within 60 days of the time he took office he would appoint a nonpartisan committee of distinguished and representative citizens to advise him on the general problem of "doing something" about the decay in the center of New Haven.

He won the election, but found it impossible to redeem his pledge within the time he had allotted himself. Several distinguished business leaders turned him down when he asked them to head his Citizens Action Commission. At least one leader declined to serve because he felt that Lee was too inexperienced to succeed. However, Lee persevered and finally persuaded a banker, Carl Freese, to become his CAC chairman. Freese in turn assisted Lee in filling the other places on the Commission. As it was finally constituted, the Commission included what Mayor Lee called the "biggest muscles" in the community: heads of most of New Haven's largest business firms, two representatives of Yale, three high-ranking bank officers, labor leaders, manufacturers, utility officers, Yankee Protestants, Italian and Irish Catholics, Jews, the leader of the Democratic party, and prominent Republicans (though no local Republican party officials).

This group was buttressed by numerous subject-matter subcommittees which drew heavily from the bipartisan, ethnically diverse population of civic activists throughout the greater New Haven area.

The influence of this conglomeration of economic, status, ethnic, and civic leaders on the making of urban redevelopment policies was negligible. But the CAC performed several significant functions. It acted as a sounding board for proposals which the city administration wished to try out before announcing them to the general public. It helped to sell the urban redevelopment program by opinion leadership within the various groups in the community. Finally, its nonpartisan quasi-official status gave the program an aura of having been "cleared" with "the people" and of being "above politics."

The Citizens Action Commission was an invention of great usefulness in assuring the political acceptability of urban redevelopment. But the Commission itself was not the source of redevelopment planning. Concrete, specific plans for redevelopment, site acquisition, relocation of residents, pricing of parcels for resale, and so on were the responsibility of the Redevelopment Agency. Coordination of these plans with the master plan for the city, traffic, zoning, housing code enforcement, and a variety of other city services were supervised by the office of the Development Administrator.

This office was also an innovation of Mayor Lee's and matches in significance his elevation of redevelopment to political prominence and then to nonpartisan untouchability. The invention of the office of Development Administrator (at a substantial salary) was the device Mayor Lee used to focus his entire city administration upon redevelopment. The job was created for Edward Logue, an energetic, aggressive, and able lawyer-administrator, to whom Mayor Lee delegated full authority to coordinate all governmental activities bearing on maintenance of the city's physical plant *in behalf of the redevelopment program.* This last phrase is crucial, because the existence of an office such as Logue's is not uncommon in communities with much less active redevelopment programs. In New Haven, however, the Development Administrator enjoyed unique powers because of the Mayor's commitment to urban redevelopment and because of his determination to make this commitment stick throughout the entire city administration.

The major substantive decisions on urban redevelopment were made by Logue, Lee, and H. Ralph Taylor, executive director of the Redevelopment Agency. Most of these decisions were made in secret. As one official said, the redevelopment program, like a submarine, "surfaced" only when it was legally or politically necessary to receive approval from the Board of Aldermen, the Redevelopment Agency, or the CAC. Our research group was unable to find a single case where this approval was not forthcoming.

Descriptions of CAC meetings were illuminating on this point. While few CAC members were willing to concede that they were a rubber stamp for the Mayor, we were able to uncover only a very few trivial instances in which modifications were made in plans presented by city technicians. More typical behavior was described to us by a CAC member in these words:

Well, the matter was taken up by the Mayor at a meeting of the Citizens Action Commission. It was discussed and debated around and we agreed with the Mayor. He got his information, of course, from the traffic commission, from the engineers, from the Redevelopment Agency and all the others and he passed it on to us. We represent the group through which these decisions are filtered. I've often felt that the group as a group is inadequate in the sense that we don't really initiate anything as far as I can recall. We haven't yet initiated anything that I know of. We discuss what has been developed by the Redevelopment Agency or the City

Planning Commission or one of the other groups. The Mayor or somebody from one of these groups presents it to us and we discuss it, we analyze it, we modify some of it, we change—

Could you give me an example of some case where you modified or changed some proposal?

Well, I don't think that I can give you an example of anything where I can say that the Commission actually changed a proposal.

You can't?

No. I say actually changed—I don't recall any.

This does not mean that the Mayor, Logue, and Taylor were able to proceed without any constraints. In fact, decision-making in redevelopment was governed by a rather comprehensive set of constraints imposed on decision-makers from the outside. Many could be stretched or neutralized, but only by the application of a variety of rather esoteric skills—in negotiation with redevelopers, in the filling out of federal forms, in the gerrymandering of project areas, and so on. Hence the significance of these constraints varied from project to project. It would, I think, be incorrect to conclude that because Lee, Logue, and Taylor succeeded in surmounting many of these obstacles with ease they could not easily have stymied a less able or ambitious city administration.

First, rather strict rules and regulations were prescribed by the Housing and Home Finance Agency which granted the federal share of the costs of redevelopment programs. These regulations covered such items as (1) whether the area to be redeveloped was sufficiently deteriorated to fall under the federal program, (2) how the city planned to finance its share of the program, (3) whether the parcel to be redeveloped was suitably shaped and sized for reuse according to accepted planning practices, (4) whether the reuse plan submitted by the city conformed to the city's master plan and to good planning practices and was economically promising, (5) whether the proper clearances had been received from competent local authorities.

Secondly, the programs had to be economically feasible. Federal grants for urban redevelopment pay for planning and subsidize the city sufficiently so that it can buy properties, knock down buildings, and sell land at a loss to redevelopers. But the city must find redevelopers willing to risk their capital while staying within the strictures of a reuse plan that can be approved by the federal government.

Other economic problems relate to the retention of industries in the community. Suppose a large industrial establishment wishes to be included in a redevelopment area but is not, or wishes to be excluded but is slated for demolition. The city may run the risk of losing the industry unless it makes an attempt to accommodate to the firm's wishes. But suppose in order to accommodate the firm the federal rules of eligibility for a project are stretched? In such a case the whole project is jeopardized. Calculations of economic feasibility thus play a substantial part in determining the content of urban redevelopment proposals.

A third set of constraints involves political questions. One general political constraint which the New Haven redevelopment decision-makers felt heavily was the dread of having to raise taxes in order to meet the city's share of the cost of redevelopment. This political problem strained the ingenuity of planners to the limit. Their problem was in part to find ways of justifying to the federal government, as contributions toward the city's share of the costs, expenditures which the city had to make sooner or later anyway, and in part to find money in other ways, such as by raising assessments on real estate on a piecemeal basis.

Another political constraint—the necessity of obtaining clearance from the Board of Aldermen—was not a serious problem during the period of our study owing to Mayor Lee's overwhelming Democratic majority on the Board.

Still another political constraint was exercised by actors in the community: owners of properties to be acquired, for example, who had resources sufficient to tie the redevelopment program up in the courts. Acquisition costs and reuse plans had to a certain extent to be accommodated to these interests.

Throughout, as a general protection against litigation, an airtight case had to be presented at public hearings for each separate project. Supporters had to be mobilized. The conservative, anti-Lee newspapers had to be watched, and if possible kept at bay. Finally, and most importantly, Mayor Lee's political popularity, as measured by his electoral majorities, could not be jeopardized. All of these political problems entered into decisions on the content and timing of plans.

On the whole, opposition to the urban redevelopment program and its component projects was slight. The community consensus favoring the program was widespread and the level of saliency on the community political agenda was high. The Mayor, his appointees in the city government, and his allies in the community were mainly responsible for this. External factors favoring the program included the availability of federal funds and a general sense among many responsible New Haven citizens that it was appropriate to "do something" about their decaying downtown area. But these conditions existed in many communities having small redevelopment programs or none. Many constraints operated on decision-makers in this area, but substantial innovations in political organization, public opinion-making, municipal administration, and in the physical landscape were effected by virtue of the ingenuity, hard work, skill, and expertise of the Mayor and his principal assistants.[5]

PUBLIC EDUCATION

In spite of the fact that as many as one-fifth of New Haven's school children are educated in private or parochial schools, the public school system of the city is by far the largest item in the municipal budget.[6] The determination of policy in this issue-area would be important if only because of the sheer size of the city's school system in comparison with other city services. But in addition the schools have great importance in any community as the major public agency which transmits to the young salient facts about the adult society. Hence a variety of valued outcomes are routinely distributed by decisions made in the area of public education. These outcomes do not relate exclusively to the distribution of jobs and money, but also to what is often loosely and somewhat melodramatically termed "control over the minds of the young."

During the years we were studying New Haven, several significant events in public education took place, including the sale of the city's two high schools and the erection of two new high schools, the appointment of a new assistant superintendent, and the emergence on several occasions of the previously uninfluential Board of Education as an important force in the process of policy-making.

New Haven's school system has a pyramidal table of organization, not unlike that of any large bureaucratic organization. The number and diversity of decisions made within this organization must, in the aggregate, be staggering. Thousands of students are placed, scheduled, tested, graded, promoted, and graduated. Truants are identified and pursued, or not. Textbooks are adopted or rejected. Teachers are hired, trans-

5. I am not, of course, assessing the "goodness" in any sense of the New Haven urban redevelopment plan nor am I suggesting that the plan will or will not succeed in doing what its proponents have hoped it would do.

6. See Dahl, *Who Governs?*, Chap. 11.

ferred, and promoted. And so on. Most of these decisions are, needless to say, decentralized and have only limited consequences. Hence a convenient way to begin a description of the "normal political process" in this issue-area would be to indicate that, as far as we know, the vast preponderance of decisions in the school system were made more or less according to the prescriptions implied in its organization chart. The most significant actor in most public education issues was therefore the superintendent of schools.[7]

In what ways did major decisions in public education reflect significant deviations from this pattern? Perhaps the most conspicuous deviations had to do with the sale and rebuilding of high schools, since these decisions were made primarily outside the organizational hierarchy of the school system.

New Haven's two high schools and a vocational school, all badly run down, were located in a downtown enclave completely surrounded by Yale University. Yale authorities were finding it quite difficult to acquire land for expansion, and the land the high schools occupied was from their point of view an especially desirable parcel. They were also concerned about the ever-present threat to precarious town-gown relations posed by the daily movement of high school students through Yale precincts on their way to and from school. Thus Yale's needs complemented the city's rather well. From either standpoint, the sale of this land was logical.

The main actor in this series of decisions was the Mayor. He proposed to the president of Yale that the university buy the old high schools. He conducted the major share of the negotiations on the price

7. Students of bureaucratic decision-making have repeatedly shown that workers in bureaucratic organizations quite often behave in ways which are not formally prescribed and which change significantly the goals their agencies actually seek. See, for example, Peter Blau, *The Dynamics of Bureaucracy* (Chicago, Univ. of Chicago Press, 1955); Blau, *Bureaucracy in Modern Society* (New York, Random House, 1956); James G. March and Herbert A. Simon, *Organizations* (New York, Wiley, 1958); Alvin Gouldner, *Patterns of Industrial Bureaucracy* (Glencoe, Free Press, 1954); Robert K. Merton et al., *Reader in Bureaucracy* (Glencoe, Free Press, 1952).

We did not conduct our research in New Haven in such a way that we could ascertain the extent to which people below the top levels of the school system had modified the outcomes of the system by emphasizing some aspects of their jobs and ignoring others. Evidence gathered in other bureaucracies suggests that some of this was going on in the New Haven school system but how much change or what kinds of changes were being introduced, I cannot say. In the appendix to this chapter I discuss how this gap in our research (i.e. the fact that we failed to study all but "major" decisions) bears on the question of the confidence that can be placed in the conclusions our study reached.

of the property. He participated actively in negotiations with the semi-autonomous Park Board on the location of the new schools, and, with his Development Administrator, made several significant decisions about the plans for the new buildings themselves.

The Mayor has, formally, only one vote out of eight on the Board of Education, although he appoints the other members to fixed terms of office (whose duration exceeds his own). In the protracted and arduous negotiations over the schools, the Mayor had the acquiescence of the entire Board, and the especially strong support of two members whom he had himself originally appointed.

These members—a Yale professor and a labor union leader (later joined by a headquarters official of a national educational organization) —formed a coalition within the Board; on a variety of issues they attempted to take certain initiatives they felt would improve the operation of the school system. There was a general feeling among them that the superintendent of schools had not surrounded himself with the ablest top assistants available; that, rather, in his promotions policy, he placed more emphasis on loyalty to him than on general competence. On the initiative of the new coalition, the Board took several steps which brought it into conflict with the superintendent.

The most important of these from the standpoint of the Board was the appointment of an assistant superintendent who was quite independent of the superintendent in her attitudes and professional commitments and who enjoyed high standing in her own right professionally and in the community. On the next most important issue, an attempt by the Board activists to change and to regularize promotions policy to a greater degree, the proposed plan failed to receive the support of the leading teachers' union and was not adopted.

The existence of two teachers' unions, a custodians' union, and a principals' association, and the close involvement of the leaders of these groups in both educational policy recommendations and election-year bargaining with public officials, suggests the possibility of other deviations from strict hierarchy in decision-making through the activity of interest groups. The appointment of a high official of one of the unions to an important post in one of the high schools occasioned unfavorable comment in the community during the course of our research. A more significant indication of the role of the unions in educational policy-making was the rejection of the personnel scheme proposed by the Mayor's close allies on the Board of Education. The activities of the teachers' unions are also alleged by many close observers of the city's politics to have been decisive in electing Mayor Lee's predecessor, William Celentano, in 1945.

One kind of decision in the school system seems especially vulnerable to interest-group activity. This is the hiring, transfer, and promotion of personnel. Factional alignments within the school hierarchy, the unions, and (for top-level vacancies) the Board of Education play a part in the determination of personnel policy. In addition, the leaders of New Haven's political parties have been known to take a rather persistent interest in the outcomes of personnel decisions, with varying degrees of success. The intervention of political leaders in personnel policy is no doubt related to a desire to do favors for political allies in order to build and maintain their political strength, and so it may be that party leaders are themselves, to a certain extent, transmitting pressures they are receiving from the leaders of ethnic voting groups in the community for "proper" representation in the upper echelons of the school system.

While the ethnic groups seem to be more interested in personnel than other kinds of policy, other interest groups also focus their attention on different aspects of school policy. At least one local PTA was able to force improvements of its school, and the unions have concerned themselves with general levels of compensation and work rules. The activities of these organizations have not been confined to formalities such as collective bargaining, but have also extended explicitly into attempts to mobilize public opinion and to influence the outcomes of elections. City administrations have, at least since 1945, found it expedient to attend to the preferences expressed by these groups, for fear of consequences at the next election.

Most decisions in public education, then, were made by educational administrators, more or less hierarchically. A set of particularly significant decisions was made in a process of negotiation in which the Mayor was the central figure. Other sets of significant decisions were made by means of negotiations within the Board of Education, among a cohesive group on the Board, the superintendent and miscellaneous interest groups, and between the Board and the superintendent, and still other decisions were made by negotiation between party leaders and educational administrators.

POLITICAL NOMINATIONS

Public officials, as we have seen, played significant roles in community decision-making in New Haven. But how did these public officials come to occupy the positions which made it possible for them to have an impact on outcomes? Most of the public officials mentioned thus far were appointed to office, and most of the appointments were made by the mayor, who is elected every two years.

New Haven's charter provides for a "weak mayor" form of government in which the chief executive is constitutionally constrained in three ways. First, legislation and the budget must be approved by the Board of Aldermen, a body of elective officials who represent each of the thirty-three wards of New Haven. Secondly, many executive prerogatives are vested in semi-autonomous boards and commissions whose members are appointed by the mayor for fixed terms, usually longer than his own. The mayor is normally an *ex officio* member of each of these boards, but he is not a member of the Board of Aldermen. Thirdly, some executive responsibilities devolve upon lesser city officials who are also elected bi-annually: the city treasurer, the city clerk, the registrar of vital statistics, and so on.

In practice, the office of the mayor provides great opportunities for an ambitious and popular incumbent to be as strong as he likes. The many boards and commissions provide the mayor with numerous opportunities to make appointments with a variety of ends in view. He can use his powers of appointment to make friends and mend fences, to further policies he favors, or to confer honors. In addition, the mayor has many other indulgences and deprivations at his command. Many millions of dollars in contracts for insurance, for snow removal and garbage collection, for printing, and so on move through various agencies under the mayor's aegis. The laws may be enforced rigidly or leniently. City agencies may hire, transfer, and discharge personnel.

Obviously the manipulatability of outcomes from the mayor's office varies from case to case, and a variety of informal constraints reduces the likelihood that all conceivable opportunities will be grasped by any one mayor; nonetheless the opportunities are there. No other city official enjoys comparable opportunities, although the city courts, which are appointed by the governor, also distribute indulgences. These are allocated in New Haven mostly in accordance with the wishes of the local political leader, John Golden.

The extent to which public officials distribute the indulgences of their offices autonomously has for years been a matter of some interest to students of politics.[8] In New Haven, it appears that most elected

8. The literature on presidential appointments to high-level office is most intriguing on this point. Dean Mann and Jameson Doig of the Brookings Institution are currently conducting a large-scale historical study of presidential appointments in order to

officials are granted nomination on the condition that the patronage of their office will be placed at the disposal of the party leaders instrumental in nominating them. This was not the case with Mayor Lee, who cooperated on equal terms with his party leader, John Golden, but his autonomy has been a temporary phenomenon earned by smashing successes at the polls in 1957 and 1959. A public official said in 1962, after an election in which Lee's majority was sharply reduced, "This patronage thing ebbs and flows. Now they don't go to [Mayor Lee] so much, but they're more likely to go to John Golden for favors."

If public office is a base of influence of major significance in determining the outcomes of public policy, then the process of nominating public officials is likewise of major significance. Both major parties in New Haven are well organized and normally have a fighting chance in every election. That is, a popular candidate running on either ticket has a good chance of winning—a circumstance which is not typical of American cities.

New Haven is an ethnically diverse community. The largest minority groups are composed of the children and grandchildren of Irish and Italian immigrants. The Irish appear to predominate in the Democratic party, and the Italians in the Republican. Both parties, however, take pains to appeal to both groups.[9] A typical city ticket for either party will have Irish, Italian, Jewish, Polish, Yankee, and Negro "names" on it. There appears to be a slight tendency for the smaller ethnic groups to pre-empt minor places on the ticket. For example, someone of Polish descent is customarily nominated for sheriff.

Although ethnic segregation is declining, New Haven's population is still clustered residentially more or less according to ethnic groups, and the ward political organizations and nominees for aldermen reflect these clusters. Temporary variations from this pattern occasionally occur, as, for example, when Negroes move into previously white areas but the ward committee continues to nominate white aldermen.

---

answer some of the questions about the actual extent of presidential autonomy raised by Hoover Commission proposals for a senior civil service and strong academic objections that this would harm the political position of the President. For highlights of this debate see George A. Graham, "The Presidency and the Executive Office of the President," *Journal of Politics*, 12 (Nov. 1950), 599–621; Stephen K. Bailey, "The President and His Political Executives," *The Annals*, 307 (Sept. 1956), 24–36; Wallace S. Sayre, "The Presidency and the Political Executives" (mimeo.) delivered at the Conference on the Political Executive, Woodrow Wilson School, Princeton, N.J., March 1956; James W. Fesler, "Administrative Literature and the Second Hoover Commission Reports," *Am. Pol. Sci. Rev.*, 51 (March 1957), 135–57.

9. Dahl, *Who Governs?*, pp. 38–39, 45–46, 110, 216–17.

The first general point that can be made is that most political nominations are determined by the logic of the situation described above. Prospective candidates must display an ethnic membership appropriate for the office they aspire to. Which ethnic group gets which office depends on the competitive situation between the parties and the probable distribution of offices among prospects on the rest of the party slate. Secondly, the prospective candidate must be "deserving," that is, unusually well qualified for the office, or especially well liked, or, no doubt most important, a party worker. Some combination of all of these factors enters into party slate-making. Mayor Lee's own nomination reflected this process. He had worked his way up through the ranks, joining the party at an early age and participating in party work over many years. Although he came from mixed Irish, Scottish, and English ancestry, for public and party purposes he referred to himself as Irish, the predominant ethnic strain in the New Haven Democratic party. Some years ago, Lee sided with party leader John Golden in a particularly serious intraparty fight, and thereafter Golden assisted Lee's advancement to a position of leadership on the Board of Aldermen and subsequently to candidacy for mayor.

How are the varying claims of competing aspirants for public office adjudicated? Who determines the actual party slate and selects the strategy of appeal to the voters which the slate implies? For the Democratic party, during the years of our study, this process rested almost wholly with three men; John Golden (Democratic national committeeman), Mayor Lee, and Arthur T. Barbieri (Democratic town chairman).

Each of these men had somewhat independent, though overlapping, bases of power: Golden had old and close connections throughout the party organization, including ties with the courts and statewide and up-county party leaders; Lee had great popularity with the electorate, which he nourished by exercising his considerable skills in public relations, and he controlled the city administration, with its several hundred patronage appointments annually and millions of dollars in contracts of various kinds; and Barbieri, the weakest of the three, dispensed a great deal of patronage directly as managing head of the party organization, a position he attained through Lee and Golden. Differences in temperament, age, background, and political support among these three men made policy disagreements among them possible—indeed even probable—on many occasions. But none of the three seems to have desired a showdown, especially over a trivial matter—and most matters were likely to be defined as trivial by successful politicians as interdependent as these three.

They were known to have split on some policy issues; Barbieri, for example, is supposed to have been responsible for the defeat of a charter reform referendum, which Lee favored, in 1955, and Golden opposed a charter proposal backed by Lee in 1958.[10] In general, however, the three leaders worked out a pattern of consultation. Golden and Barbieri were largely indifferent to policy questions, except as they affected elections and contracts. This left a broad but vague zone of indifference within which Lee could determine the policies of the party in New Haven. Lee seldom found it worthwhile to back policies distasteful to the other two, since he could innovate in so many areas without provoking their opposition. Candidate selection is one area of great importance to the morale of the organization, but, except for the position of mayor, has limited policy consequences. The party organization treated nomination for office as a kind of patronage; election to offices other than mayor and probate judge did not confer on the office-holder any independence of the party organization in dispensing the patronage normally attached to the office. For these reasons, all three leaders could afford to allow the process of candidate selection to become a quasi-technical problem of putting together a ticket that would maximize appeals to the electorate and maintain the good will of rank-and-file party workers by following the well-known rules propounded above.

While the Democratic party leadership during 1957–59 consisted of a peaceable coalition, New Haven Republicans presented a somewhat more disorganized picture. There was definite rivalry between Frank Lynch, the "old" boss whose local power was based on his connections with past Republican governors and the state party leadership, and William Celentano, an ex-mayor who not unexpectedly enjoyed great personal popularity among New Haven's very large segment of Italian Republican voters. In 1958 Lynch controlled more wards, but Celentano, in coalition with the leader of his faction, George DiCenzo, controlled one entire senatorial district. Celentano was the strongest Republican mayoralty candidate, and this was the major base of his power. In a variety of instances, these two factions found it difficult to compose their differences. Lynch felt Celentano failed to cooperate sufficiently with him in dispensing City Hall patronage when Celentano was mayor. This was no doubt true since Lynch opposed Celentano's nomination

10. Discussed in detail in Wolfinger, *The Politics of Progress.*

as mayor in 1945, the year Celentano succeeded in overturning the Democratic regime of Mayor Murphy. Celentano felt that Lynch was equally at fault for not letting him share state patronage during John Lodge's term as governor. Celentano also felt that Lynch failed to boost him for lieutenant governor with the state leadership.

Celentano refused steadfastly to run against the extremely popular Mayor Lee, apparently preferring to wait until Lee moved on to higher office. Lynch and his ally, Republican town chairman Henry DeVita, were unable to find a candidate for mayor who could beat Lee, and the Celentano forces probably worked covertly against Republican nominees for mayor in order to enhance Celentano's intraparty position. Needless to say, Lee encouraged the DiCenzo-Celentano segment of the Republican party, which considered his success (and, hopefully, his subsequent movement out of New Haven city politics) a prerequisite to its own.

THE STRATIFICATION THEORY REVISITED

We now return to the five key propositions of the stratification theory. Are these propositions useful in analyzing information about policy-making in New Haven? Or, alternatively, what does a description of policy-making processes in New Haven suggest about the relevance of the five propositions?

First, did an economic or status elite make significant decisions in any of the three issue-areas studied? Obviously the answer depends on the definition of the term "economic or status elite." As we have seen, no uniform criteria for inclusion in these elites are specified in the literature, nor are elites even defined as necessarily having any particular size. These are matters of some inconvenience to a student who wishes to make an independent test of the stratification theory. If we cannot be sure what the criteria for inclusion in the elite group are, then we cannot be sure whether any particular individual satisfies these criteria, and the theory can never be substantiated or disproved. I shall proceed, however, under the assumption that, as social scientists, stratification theorists value empirical validation of their theories, and so I shall suggest criteria that can be used to identify members of New Haven's economic and social "elites."

The definition of "economic elite" to be used here is an adaptation of the definition Schulze used in his stratification analysis of Cibola.[11] For

11. Schulze's criteria for determining the composition of the economic elite are the most inclusive of any stratification study that describes operations for identifying an

the purposes of studying New Haven, let us assume that the economic leaders of the community are to be found among the following groups: (1) the president and chairman of the board of every company having a total assessed evaluation putting it among the city's top 50 taxpayers during any of the five years 1953–58; (2) any individual whose total assessed evaluation during the years 1957 or 1958 was greater than $250,000; (3) the presidents and chairmen of the board of all banks and utilities; (4) any individual who was a director of a New Haven bank or of three or more local corporations having an assessment of $250,000 or more or employing more than 50 if a manufacturer, or employing more than 25 if a retailer.[12] These four criteria yield a list of 239 names, which we may take as a suitable "economic elite" for the purposes of our study.

Who are the status elite? The New Haven *Blue Book,* a privately published social register last issued in 1951, identifies some 2,000 families.[13] In this book special mention is made of the names of the "Cotillion Set," the group of families which subscribed to the Assembly of the New Haven Lawn Club in that year. This Cotillion list is published annually in the New Haven *Register.* All families subscribing in 1951, 1958, or 1959 may be considered members of the social status elite, a list of 231 names after duplicates are stricken.[14]

We may now inquire: can any of the major participants in the issue-areas just described be found on either of these lists? The answer is yes.

In the field of public education, A. Whitney Griswold, president of Yale and a member of both economic and status elites, agreed in behalf of Yale to purchase the old high schools. The detailed negotiations were carried forward by others, however. The purchase of the high schools afforded political opponents of Mayor Lee the opportunity to charge that the Mayor was controlled by Yale interests. Lee, although

economic elite. The criteria used here are even more inclusive than Schulze's. See Schulze, "The Role of Economic Dominants in Community Power Structure," *Am. Soc. Rev., 23* (Feb. 1958), 3–9. This definition has previously been used in my article, "Three Problems in the Analysis of Community Power," *Am. Soc. Rev., 24* (Dec. 1959), 796–803, and in Dahl, *Who Governs?,* p. 67.

12. The President of Yale University, one of the three largest employers in New Haven, is included in the list of economic leaders, although he meets none of the criteria for inclusion since Yale is not a manufacturer or a retailer, or as heavy a taxpayer as it would be if its land were put to commercial uses.

13. New Haven, 1951.

14. The temptation would ordinarily be great to use all 2,000 families in the *Blue Book* as the status elite. The decision to use the somewhat more restricted Cotillion list is based on the availability of Cotillion lists during the years 1958 and 1959, at which point the *Blue Book* was almost a decade out of date.

not a college man himself, had been director of the Yale News Bureau before he became mayor and was known to prize highly his social connections with members of the Yale faculty and administration.[15] However, Lee's surface vulnerability on this point seemed to inspire him to lean over backward in his dealings with the university. A substantial city tax assessment was slapped on Yale's handsome new hockey rink. Yale's attempts to purchase redevelopment land from the city for middle-income faculty apartments were balked by stringent conditions set by the Mayor. And, on the high schools, Mayor Lee asked and received an extremely high price, three million dollars. A Yale official once said, "as the university sees it . . . we paid the city more for those schools than either they were worth intrinsically or than the city could have got from any other purchaser."

Members of the social elite appear in another connection in the area of public education. When Mayor Lee decided to sell the high schools, it became necessary to locate land on which to build new high schools. The problem of cost pointed to park land as the solution, so it became necessary for the Board of Education to ask the Park Board to release some land for this purpose. Protracted negotiations ensued over what park land this was to be.

While all the boards in New Haven's government are to a certain extent autonomous, the Park Board is especially so because it consists in part of the high-status descendants of donors of park land to the city, who sit on the Board by legal right. Thus several high-status individuals, by virtue of their membership on the Park Board, participated significantly in the negotiations over the location of the new high schools.

The Board of Education asked for two sites which they thought were ideally located. An even more important consideration was that these sites, Edgewood Park on the west and Rice Field on the east, would require little or no expensive site preparation. The Park Board refused to give up these locations, however, and proposed alternative sites. The Board of Education, on the advice of the Mayor, accepted Beaver Pond in the west, hoping for a concession by the Park Board on the eastern

15. A stratification analyst, Floyd Hunter, has referred to Lee as a businessman-mayor in a review of Dahl, *Who Governs?*, in *Administrative Science Quarterly, 6* (March 1962), 517–19. It may be well in view of this to quote Dahl (p. 118) on Lee's background: "He came from a Catholic working-class family of mixed English, Scottish and Irish origins . . . went to New Haven public schools, worked as a reporter on the *Journal Courier,* served as an officer in the Junior Chamber of Commerce, had a brief spell in the army, and from 1943 until his election as mayor was in charge of Yale's public relations."

location. Instead the Park Board suggested three possibilities in succession. The first abutted a rundown and patently undesirable neighborhood. The second would have wiped out a large section of the most used park land in the city and would have provoked a great outcry. The third alternative, which the Board of Education finally accepted with reluctance, was a rather swampy wasteland which required over a million dollars in site preparation before construction could begin. This was unquestionably a major defeat for the Mayor and the Board of Education.

Finally, one of Mayor Lee's appointees to the Board of Education was a member of the status elite. This was Maynard Mack, professor of English at Yale. Mack was recruited to educational policy-making when he became active in the PTA in the neighborhood grammar school where three of his children were enrolled. The physical condition of this particular school was, in his words, "really dreadful," so parents in the area formed a committee to persuade the city to rehabilitate the school. This movement coincided with an election campaign, with the result that many improvements were actually made in the school building. As a PTA president and a leader in this controversy, Mack came to Mayor Lee's attention, and when Lee was elected and formed a Citizens Advisory Council for Education—a forerunner of other citizens action committees—Mack was asked to join. About six months after Mayor Lee took office in 1953, two seats on the school board fell vacant. In one case a member's term had expired, and in the other the Mayor succeeded in forcing a sitting member to resign. Mack and a labor leader, Mitchell Sviridoff, were then appointed to the Board, where they formed the nucleus of the activist coalition described earlier.

In urban redevelopment, several members of the economic or status elite performed vital tasks in aid of the Mayor. In particular, the bankers Carl Freese and Frank O'Brion (who headed the Redevelopment Agency) were instrumental in soliciting the support or at least the acquiescence of business leaders, a few of whom were opposed to the urban redevelopment program. Freese's successor as chairman of the CAC, utility executive Lucius Rowe, also actively supported the redevelopment program. Rowe was especially vigorous in his support of the main precondition of the program's continued success, namely, the continued electoral success of Mayor Lee. As many as 15 per cent of the names appearing on the literature of the Citizens Action Commission as members of the Commission or subsidiary committees could also be found on the list of the economic or status elite, but very few members of the

CAC—economic and social leader or not—had any direct individual importance in the shaping of redevelopment decisions.

In the field of political nominations, one leader's name appears as a member of the economic elite. Surprisingly enough, this was not a Republican,[16] but John Golden, long-time "boss" of New Haven's Democratic party. Golden's appearance in this connection is instructive because it illustrates one possible relation between political and economic achievement not stressed by the stratification analysis.[17] For Golden's high economic standing was achieved as a result of activities and alliances built up over a long period of time in politics. Golden has devoted his life to politics. He began life as the son of Catholic working-class parents. His first job was at the Greist Manufacturing Company where he rose to superintendent. He was active in ward politics and civic organizations and in due course was appointed director of public works by Mayor Murphy, after which he set up his own insurance brokerage firm. Golden's political connections have over the years thrown him into contact with a great many prospective clients, and his insurance business has prospered. Golden is now a well-to-do man. He appears on the list of the economic notables because he is a director of a New Haven bank, the smallest in the community, established by a few of his political allies. This bank is run by Democrats and Jews, and it stands well outside the major financial circles of New Haven. The larger savings banks in New Haven frequently interlock in their directorates with the larger commercial banks (and appear systematically to exclude both Jews and Democrats), but no board member of this small bank has ever participated in such an arrangement.

It would be difficult to conclude from this recitation that an elite of high status or great wealth ran New Haven, at least with respect to those issues in community life which were subjected to investigation. On the other hand, economic and status leaders were not wholly excluded from participation. Rather, as in the case of members of other New Haven groups, some participated, but most did not.

Were political and civic leaders in some sense subordinated to the upper class? An affirmative answer would require us to find:

1. That members of the upper class customarily gave orders to political and civic leaders and that these orders subsequently were carried out,

16. Several Republican economic leaders whom we interviewed mentioned that they were active in politics in one or another of the suburban towns surrounding New Haven.

17. Cf. Dahl, *Who Governs?*, pp. 72–75.

or 2. That when members of the upper class opposed policies of political and civic leaders they regularly got their way,

or 3. That members of the upper class controlled to some significant extent the chances of political leaders to become leaders, that is, that in some sense they placed their people in positions of leadership.

These powers could not, of course, be shared widely with others in the community or the proposition would have to be rejected.

One of the most striking things about Mayor Lee's urban redevelopment program was his ability to induce economic and status leaders of top rank in the community to "front" for the activities of the professional redevelopment staff. I have noted the persistent claim by stratification writers studying other communities that the "top echelon" customarily stays out of the limelight, leaving overt civic leadership to underlings.[18] In this case, the people behind the scenes were professionals in City Hall, who formulated their extensive programs largely in secret.

Mayor Lee's achievement in generating support from New Haven's economic and social elite should not be underestimated. As a Democratic mayor he had, in the first instance, to overcome the natural reluctance of upper-class Republicans to cooperate with him. But eventually economic and social leaders, who had originally been reluctant to support the urban redevelopment program, became so firmly committed to the program and to Lee that many of these lifelong Republicans found themselves actively supporting Lee for the U.S. Senate and contributing heavily to his re-election campaign against the Republican candidate. At least one businessman even suggested that the *Republican* party nominate Lee for mayor.

In the case of public education, only the success of the Park Board in the selection of the site of one of the high schools stands as an example of the power of high-status individuals. But membership on the Park Board can hardly be regarded as a command post of much lasting utility to the individual anxious to exert an influence over educational policy. Professor Maynard Mack, a high-status loser in the high school controversy, was not, as we have seen, in any sense placed on the Board by the upper class, but rather arrived there by a combination of self-propulsion and selection by Mayor Lee.

Political nominations, in a community with a competitive two-party

18. See, for example, Lynd, *MIT,* passim, esp. pp. 38–39, 97, 321; Warner, *Jonesville,* passim, esp. pp. 100, 101, 103; Hollingshead, *Elmtown,* passim, esp. p. 91; C. Wright Mills, "The Middle Classes in Middle-sized Cities," *Am. Soc. Rev., 13* (Dec. 1946), 520–29; Hunter, *CPS,* passim, esp. pp. 24, 60–114, 174.

system, is perhaps the hardest area of all for an upper-class elite to control from behind the scenes because of the demands made by party organizations for candidates who can win. As I have indicated, we could find no instance of economic or status leaders dictating political nominations to suit themselves, aside from the leadership of John Golden, who is a party man first and only incidentally a member of the economic elite.

Thus we must reject the second proposition of the stratification theory.

The remaining three propositions fare no better. Is there a single power elite in the community? In each of the three issue-areas studied, entirely different decision-making processes could be identified. In urban redevelopment, a broadly based coalition consisting of civic leaders and municipal bureaucrats headed by a democratically elected official, the mayor, undertook sweeping innovations. In public education, some outcomes were achieved through the negotiations of the mayor, some through the efforts of a group of activists on the school board, some through the demands of interest groups, and most through the day-to-day workings of the school system bureaucracy, whose most significant actor was the superintendent. Political nominations were determined in part by custom and in part by strategic considerations between factions within the parties and between the two parties. In each issue-area different actors appeared, their roles were different, and the kinds of alternatives which they had to choose among were different. A very few actors appeared in more than one issue-area. Of these by far the most important was the mayor. The others had major roles in only one issue-area and played bit parts in a second. For example, President A. Whitney Griswold agreed to buy the high schools for Yale, a major decision in public education. In urban redevelopment, President Griswold appeared as the vice-chairman of the Citizens Action Commission, where he lent his prestigeful presence to several public meetings devoted to the discussion of the program.

In order to say that New Haven was ruled by a single power elite, we must find a small group, not selected by some democratic means, which was united in its policy aims and consistently got its way in more than one significant policy area. We could not find such a group in New Haven.

Even though there was no upper-class power elite, it still might be true that the outcomes of major decisions tended nonetheless to benefit members of the upper class more than any other group, thus favoring the long-run maintenance of this group.

But this is a difficult assertion to test. For example, are all owners of land in downtown New Haven similarly situated with respect to urban redevelopment decisions? Some landowners whose property was included regretted the fact, and one fought the redevelopment program. Others regretted *not* being included, and one of these fought the program. Still others were, in varying degrees, satisfied with the situation.

Whom did the new high schools benefit? The benefits and costs to any individual of these steel-and-concrete policy outcomes are diffuse and intangible and perhaps impossible to evaluate sensibly without making all sorts of highly questionable assumptions. The same is true of most other policy outcomes.

The only outcomes presenting a less ambiguous aspect are those actively espoused by a united upper class in opposition to others in the community. But we could find no decisions where even a substantial proportion of the upper class was active, where that portion of the upper class that was active was wholly united, or where they were substantially in less agreement with members of other classes than they were among themselves.

Thus we must also reject the proposition that major social conflicts in New Haven took place between the upper class and those below. In rejecting this last of the five key propositions of stratification theory as suitable for explaining decision-making events in New Haven, must we also, as well, reject the notion that indulgences and deprivations were distributed unevenly in the community? Did no one therefore rule? Was there no social conflict?

It would, as a matter of fact, be quite impossible to disprove the assertions of the stratification theory in a situation where there was no social conflict, just as it would be impossible to prove them. In New Haven there were many conflicts, some of them quite serious. But different patterns of conflict prevailed in different policy areas.

This is perhaps easiest to see in the area of public education, where the major conflict was a subdued antagonism between the superintendent and his supporters within the system, on the one hand, and the dominant faction on the Board of Education and its supporters, on the other.

This major conflict was superimposed upon the historical remains of two others: the original alignment of factions within the school system which supported and opposed the ouster by the present superintendent of his immediate predecessor; and, secondly, a continuing struggle by professionals in the school system to free personnel policies from "meddling" by party chieftains.

Often at stake as well were concrete matters of policy in which professionals disagreed with professionals, as in a running controversy over the testing program in the elementary schools. The Board of Education divided on the question of the wholesomeness of the high schools' annual Harvest Festival. Concrete issues such as these, and the advocates of the various sides of these issues, provided the bases for the significant conflicts in the field of education. Partisans could be identified not by their status characteristics, but only by their words and deeds relevant to actual controversies in the making of educational policy.

Urban redevelopment was an issue-area in which social conflict was held to a minimum by the strenuous efforts of the Mayor and his staff. On the original slum clearance, known as the Oak Street Project, and in the renewal of the Wooster Square section, which was the third phase of the city-wide program, opposition to the Mayor's plans was slight. This was true because most members of the community were wholly apathetic until aroused and educated by the Mayor to the possibilities of urban renewal. In addition, a few leaders in the community had recognized for years that something approximating these projects would be desirable if it could be achieved; and Mayor Lee achieved it cheaply by taking advantage of federal funds. No corporate group, save a scattering of disorganized slum landlords, stood to lose from the removal of the Oak Street eyesore, and the introduction into the adjacent area of the Connecticut Turnpike and feeder roads, built this time with state funds, was used by Mayor Lee as the occasion for accomplishing this project. In order to facilitate the Oak Street slum removal, it was necessary for Mayor Lee and his redevelopment staff to persuade the state highway department to change its original proposals, so as to bring the roads into conformity with plans for redevelopment. In this sense, the Mayor not only used the Turnpike as an opportunity for redevelopment, but also created this opportunity by negotiating for an extension of feeder roads through the worst of the slum area.

The second phase of urban redevelopment, the Church Street Project, was by far the most ambitious part of the program. This project involved razing a substantial portion of the city center, in which numerous retail stores were located. A group of small merchants who were directly affected objected strenuously to being removed from their places of business. Some of them were unable to sustain the loss of good will and improvements and were forced out of business. This group never attacked the redevelopment program per se, however; they only objected to its untoward effects on themselves. The city administration attempted to handle these objections by devising palliatives. It underwrote a 10 per cent reduction on rentals offered by the redeveloper to all displaced businesses taken into the new project;[19] it set up a business relocation office which turned out to be largely ineffectual, but which was designed to assist displaced merchants in finding suitable space; and, finally, the city aided financially in the construction of temporary housing for displaced businesses on cleared land in the downtown area.

The small merchants' objections to the redevelopment program were aired primarily at public hearings. The city administration always took these public occasions seriously and generally succeeded in offsetting the testimony of dissidents by producing a tidal wave of support for the program in the form of public statements by leaders from all conceivable segments of the community: business, banking, real estate, labor, religious and human welfare civic groups, PTA's, ethnic minorities, and so on.

Other objections came from two retailers in the community, one of middling size, the other quite important. In dealing with these and one or two other economically powerful dissidents, the Mayor brought other economic leaders in on behalf of the city in private negotiations. Thus conflict in urban redevelopment found members of the upper class on both sides.

One major group in the community which was severely damaged by the success of redevelopment was the Republican party. Mayor Lee put a nonpartisan gloss on his redevelopment activities by soliciting and receiving the endorsement and support of prominent New Haven Republican businessmen. Logue ran a clean and efficient operation, generally free of the City Hall patronage system.

Republican politicians did their best to exploit dissatisfactions they could find. They charged that redevelopment plans were put through with callous and undemocratic haste. They accused the Board of Aldermen of being a rubber stamp. They criticized the sale of the high schools and of redevelopment land to Yale and attacked the city administration for delays in rebuilding on cleared land. Since party membership cuts across classes, it can be said that the rather important cleavage between Democrats and Republicans also tends to weaken the proposition that social conflict is primarily a matter of interclass warfare.

Intraparty conflict in New Haven over political nominations seldom occurred along class lines. There was sometimes disagreement over who was "entitled" to what position on a party ticket, and this conflict may

19. However, the redeveloper was not obliged (and was not likely) to take into his project all those displaced businessmen who wanted to come in—nor were the actual costs of rentals in the new project made known to the public or to the displaced merchants.

have involved representatives of different ethnic groups, but it was unthinkable in a city with New Haven's large, well-organized, ethnically diverse population for either party purposefully to alienate any substantial segment of the population.

In fact, New Haven politics shows a record of hospitality especially to the numerous members of lower-status groups, such as the Italians, who were courted in earlier years, in particular, by the Ullman brothers, long-time leaders of the Republican party.[20]

As I have indicated, conflict between and within the parties reflected cleavages between individuals having commitments to different factions rather than to different classes, and in fact even party factions often attempted to achieve as socially heterogeneous a popular following as they could possibly muster.

It is, however, fair to say that there was some residue of ethnic conflict in the slight tendency for the Irish voters to cluster in the Democratic party and the Italians in the Republican party. Nonetheless, both parties continuously strove to appeal to the entire electorate, and men of both Irish and Italian descent occupied positions of leadership in both parties.

While the Irish-Italian split was the most obvious large-scale cleavage along social lines in New Haven politics, I have the impression that stratification writers would hesitate to call intramural battles between such recent immigrants true class conflicts. They seem to have had in mind conflicts between the economic and social elite and those below, and, in this respect, the New Haven political record is almost totally barren. The only instance which may fit this theory was the contest for president of the Board of Aldermen a few years ago between two Republicans: a man of Italian extraction, who later became Republican city chairman, and a prominent Yankee.

Mayor Celentano favored the Yankee, on the ground that he was appointing a tremendous number of Italians to high posts in the city government and felt that the Yankee segment of the Republican city coalition deserved the recognition of the presidency. Republican aldermen declined to cooperate, however, and the gavel passed to the Italian candidate. In fact, what looks on the surface like a Yankee vs. Italian conflict was actually a disagreement between the Celentano–DiCenzo (mostly Italian-led) wing of the Republican party, which sponsored the Yankee, and the Lynch (mostly Irish and Yankee-led) wing of the party, which backed the Italian candidate who eventually won.

20. Dahl, *Who Governs?*, p. 39.

We must conclude, first, that the five propositions of the stratification theory were not validated by the New Haven research. Insofar as they could have been rejected, they were, I think, rejected. Moreover, they do not seem to have been overly helpful in eliciting a description of how decision-making in New Haven took place. This suggests once again a notion originally discussed in the course of the earlier close examination of the stratification studies of specific communities. It may be that in communities where the stratification theory guided research, significant decision-making events and activities were unintentionally but systematically neglected.

APPENDIX: DID THE NEW HAVEN STUDY ADEQUATELY TEST THE STRATIFICATION THEORY?

It seems appropriate at this point to digress from the main thrust of my argument long enough to consider certain methodological issues raised by this approach to the problems of testing the propositions of the stratification theory with New Haven data. There are a great many difficulties associated with making a test of this kind. The key propositions themselves change slightly in their empirical references from study to study and it may be that, despite my best efforts, I have failed to capture the intentions of some stratification writers in the operations by which I sought to validate or invalidate the propositions. In Chapter 6, a systematic comparison is made of the methods used in New Haven and the methods used by stratification writers. In this appendix, I want to deal only with the question: is the method employed here adequate to accomplish its avowed purpose of making an empirical test of the stratification theory?

I would argue that the method is adequate if certain simplifications, designed to make the propositions accessible to a test, are allowed. It is generally understood that without some sort of arbitrary simplifications research is impossible. A suitable criterion by which the adequacy of a test can be judged is whether or not the simplifications introduced by the research design seem likely to prejudice the outcomes of the research.

The first simplification I made was to stipulate that to "rule" meant to initiate, modify, veto, or in some visible manner act so as to change outcomes of selected community decisions. How were these decisions selected? Two alternative strategies initially seemed feasible. I could have designated as "rulers" of New Haven those who prevailed on "representative" decisions. In pursuing the strategy of examining "important" decisions, I imposed a drastic simplification upon the complexity of the world, but the reasons for doing so seemed compelling.

We can, I think, in principle rank decisions according to their importance by making use of one or another, or a combination, of at least four criteria:

1. How many people are affected by outcomes,
2. How many different kinds of community resources are distributed by outcomes,
3. How much in amount of resources are distributed by outcomes,
4. How drastically present community resource distributions are altered by outcomes.

Presumably decisions vary greatly in their importance, and fewer decisions will be important than unimportant. Furthermore, it is entirely possible, indeed likely, that, taken together, all "unimportant" community decisions affect more people and more resources than the few "important" community decisions. This would argue, then, that the best strategy for studying community power would have been to pick "representative" decision-making processes and study them. However, this argument leaves aside certain grave empirical difficulties. While it may be a reasonably simple matter to identify the most significant decisions in community life at any given time, the problem of assessing the comparative importance of decisions becomes hopelessly snarled as one attempts to measure the comparative importance of "middle" and "low" importance decisions whose ratings may vary only slightly one from another on a single scale or fall differently among the different criteria. In decisions of "low" importance, there is also an empirical problem of deciding what constitutes a "decision." Hence the universe of decisions is an expanding one. If this is the case, then it is in fact impossible to assess the representativeness of any given set of decisions.

If it is impossible to determine the extent to which a decision is representative of other decisions in a community, or of decisions which may come afterward, and if, as I suppose, it is about equally taxing on the researcher to study an important decision as an unimportant one, then it seems clear that it is possible to learn more about how community outcomes are achieved per unit of research resources by studying how "big" decisions are arrived at, and what the necessary and sufficient conditions are for the maintenance and change of these patterns.

This, then, is one rationale for studying "important" decisions. There seem to be no satisfactory criteria which would identify a universe of all decisions in the community so that a sample of "typical" or "representative" decisions could in principle be drawn.

The reader will recall that the goal of the New Haven study was given as "to explain certain events," identified as policy-making events. It has been pointed out to me that sometimes decisions that are *not* made are every bit as significant in determining policy outcomes as decisions that are made. Indeed, it has been suggested that non-events make more significant policy than do policy-making events. This is the kind of statement that has a certain plausibility and attractiveness but that presents truly insuperable obstacles to research. We can sound the depth of the abyss very quickly by agreeing that non-events are much more important than events, and inquiring precisely *which* non-events are to be regarded as most significant in the community. Surely not *all* of them. For every event (no matter how defined) that occurs there must be an infinity of alternatives. Then which non-events are to be regarded as significant? One satisfactory answer might be: those outcomes desired by a significant number of actors in the community but not achieved. Insofar as these goals are in some way explicitly pursued by people in the community, the method of study used in New Haven has a reasonable chance of capturing them. A wholly unsatisfactory answer would be: certain non-events stipulated by outside observers without reference to the desires or activities of community residents. This answer is unsatisfactory because it is obviously inappropriate for outsiders to pick among all the possible outcomes that did not take place a set which they regard as important but which community citizens do not. This approach is likely to prejudice the outcomes of research—as indeed, I believe I have shown it does.

Another methodological problem: assuming the findings from New Haven presented here are correct, what can we infer from them about other cities? About New Haven ten years from now? Strictly speaking, the answer is little or nothing. New Haven bears certain similarities to other cities, but our theory has not yet progressed to the point where we know with any degree of confidence *which* other similarities predict political similarities. Similarly, aside from some primitive notions of "habit" or "inertia," [21] we have little to go on which helps us predict the effects on future decision-making processes of present ones. Apparently one fact of life which must be reckoned with is the relatively rapid turnover of decision-makers in many issue-areas. For example, almost all the main actors in New Haven's urban redevelopment in 1958 had disappeared by 1962. Although Mayor Lee, the most essential actor of all, was still on the scene, who could tell how long he would remain?

Finally, are the arrangements I described a "power structure"? It seems to me arbitrary whether we call the various political processes described in New Haven a "power structure" or not. The disadvantages of doing so involve two inconvenient connotative meanings of the term: first, that power and the class or status structure of the community are linked in a certain way (i.e. the way the stratification writers describe) and, secondly, that the power distributions which prevail at the time of the study are so ingrained and likely to be repeated that they can be referred to as "structural" properties of the community's social life, that is, permanently fixed in some sense. The latter is an empirical question, but I am dubious that investigation would disclose an affirmative answer.

To conclude: if we are modest in the conclusions to be drawn from the New Haven study and if the simplifications introduced to make research possible are accepted as reasonable, then I believe the adequacy of the test of the five key propositions is demonstrated.

21. As suggested, for example, in James S. Coleman's exemplary monograph, *Community Conflict* (Glencoe, Free Press, 1957), p. 2 and passim.

5. Power and Social Stratification: Theory or Ideology?

If the key propositions of stratification theory were irrelevant and untrue in New Haven, and at the least misleading and questionable in other communities, why are they so widely used, defended, and "discovered" in community studies? It is not enough to say that these other community studies are wrong, because, although this may be the case, it is also true that they are all wrong in the same or closely similar ways. This phenomenon invites investigation, for social science demands not merely identification of errors, but, if possible, the diagnosis and correction of these errors in future research.

In this chapter, three possible explanations will be advanced for the fact that the political theory of so many students of community power led them seriously astray. One explanation is that their political tastes and preferences made them want to believe that the five key propositions were true of American communities, and they were therefore victims of their personal biases. Another explanation holds that the basic axioms and presuppositions of stratification theory are such that the five key propositions can be deduced logically from them, so that by accepting the basic axioms of stratification theory researchers were unwittingly led to accept the five propositions. A third line of argument, supplementary to the second, holds that researchers were deceived by the entire intellectual framework of stratification theory. This explanation suggests that, embedded in the literature of social stratification, there are criteria governing the applicability of stratification analysis to society, and, by violating these criteria, students of community power made it highly probable that their findings would be faulty.

Let us consider the third explanation first. We can treat stratification theory, in its broadest outline, as an intellectual perspective which views society as an organism analogous in its structure to a layer cake. Writers on social stratification discuss such matters as who belongs in what layer and why, what goes on in each layer, and what relations are like between people in different layers. Stratification itself refers to the distributions of values in society. The way in which these values are distributed is critical: inequalities must exist, and, more than that, must persist if we are to say that stratification has taken place in a social system. Let us examine the rules of stratification analysis implied in this characterization.

We can think of values as things or events desired by individuals and groups in society. The values most often employed in modern stratification analysis are variants of the following three: life chances, prestige, and power. It is asserted—and, where not asserted, implied—in stratification analysis that these three values are distributed unequally in society, that they can be quantified at least roughly by the observer, and that individuals, or at least "classes" of individuals, are ordered transitively with respect to their possession of each value, so that it can be said that if A has more of value X than B and B than C, then A has more of value X than C. This third step gives an element of the stability mentioned above; it is also presumed in stratification analysis that everyone in a nuclear family will enjoy the same value-position with respect to each value and that these value-positions will tend to be passed on from generation to generation in the same family.[1]

1. Some of the general and theoretical works from which these criteria are drawn include Bernard Barber, *Social Stratification* (New York, Harcourt, Brace, 1957); Walter Buckley, "Social Stratification and Social Differentiation," *Am. Soc. Rev.*, 23 (Aug. 1958), 369–75; Reinhard Bendix and Seymour Martin Lipset, eds., *Class, Status and Power* (Glencoe, Free Press, 1953); John F. Cuber and William F. Kenkel, *Social Stratification in the United States* (New York, Appleton, 1954); Kingsley Davis, *Human Society* (New York, Macmillan, 1949); Davis and Wilbert E. Moore, "Some Principles of Stratification," *Am. Soc. Rev.*, 10 (April 1945), 242–49; Hans H. Gerth and C. Wright Mills, *Character and Social Structure* (New York, Harcourt, Brace, 1953); Milton M. Gordon, *Social Class in American Sociology* (Durham, Duke Univ. Press, 1958); Gordon, "A System of Social Class Analysis," *Drew Univ. Bulletin, 39* (Madison, N.J., Aug. 1951); Paul K. Hatt, "Social Stratification in the Mass Society," *Am. Soc. Rev.*, 15 (April 1950), 216–22; Joseph A. Kahl, *The American Class Structure* (New York, Rinehart, 1957); Harold F. Kaufman, Otis Dudley Duncan, Neal Gross, and William A. Sewell, "Problems of Theory and Method in the Study of Social Stratification in Rural Society," *Rural Sociology, 18* (March 1953), 12–24; Kurt B. Mayer, *Class and Society* (Garden City, Doubleday, 1955); Mayer, "The Theory of Social Classes," *Harvard Educational Review, 23* (Summer 1953), 149–67; Harold W. Pfautz, "The Current Literature on Social Stratification: Critique and Bibliography," *Am. J. Soc.*, 58 (Jan. 1953), 391–418; Harold W. Pfautz, "Social Stratification and Sociology," *Transactions of the Second World Congress of Sociology, 2* (1954), 311–20; Edward A. Shils, *The Present State of American Sociology* (Glencoe, Free Press, 1948); Melvin W. Tumin, "Some Principles of Stratification," *Am. Soc. Rev., 18* (Aug. 1953) (and Replies and Comments from Davis and Moore), pp. 387–97; Barber, Davis and Moore, and Talcott Parsons (in Bendix and Lipset, *Class, Status, and Power,* pp. 92–128) represent a school of theory which attempts to explain relative stabilities in the unequal prestige rankings of socially differentiated positions by positing a socially functional system

These are presumptions about empirical reality, hence criteria are immediately available for judging the conditions under which stratification analysis is appropriate. That is, insofar as conditions in the real world actually approximate the characteristics imputed to them by stratification analysts, the discussion of interclass relations and the life-styles, behavior, and attitudes of individuals as members of social classes is meaningful. But insofar as this is not the case stratification analysis may lead to great errors in describing social reality.

Let us turn to the three commonest dimensions of stratification theory and discuss briefly their appropriateness as variables in an analysis of modern American society. We shall be asking of each variable[2] in turn: (1) can it be quantified by an observer?[3] (2) is it distributed unequally in society? (3) are individuals and groups ordered transitively with respect to it? (4) does everyone in the nuclear family enjoy the same amount of it? (5) is it passed on from generation to generation in the same family?

A recent text in social stratification says of life chances:

> In modern industrial societies members of the same economic class
> have similar chances to obtain certain values and opportunities which

of rewards and penalties attaching in varying degrees to positions of more and less social responsibility and importance. Critics of this so-called "functional" approach (e.g. Buckley, Pfautz in *Transactions*, Tumin) charge that stratification implies greater stability than can be explained in this fashion; hence functionalists are explaining at most "social differentiation." Functionalists seem willing to accept this characterization cheerfully enough, if it is purged of its pejorative overtones (see Kingsley Davis, "The Abominable Heresy: A Reply to Dr. Buckley," *Am. Soc. Rev.*, 24 [Feb. 1959], 82–83). The rather more elaborate criteria of stability proposed here follow what seems to be the majority, nonfunctionalist approach; hence functionalist treatments of power are exempted from my criticism of stratification analyses at the appropriate points. I should point out, however, that functionalist treatments of power can be criticized on other grounds: e.g., they posit a central, society-wide value system according to which positions are ranked. But power in American society is decentralized in a variety of ways as, for example, by scopes (or issue-areas) and by constitutional entities, or jurisdictions; hence describing power in America by making reference to a central value system is bound to be unwieldy and inconvenient. See also Dennis H. Wrong, "The Functional Theory of Stratification: Some Neglected Considerations," *Am. Soc. Rev.*, 24 (Dec. 1959), 772–82.

2. Note that "variables" of stratification analysis are socially valued. In principle, hair color and foot size can be analyzed in the same way, but societies are not thought to be stratified on these bases because these human characteristics are not socially valued in any clearly recognizable fashion. See Robin M. Williams, Jr., *American Society* (New York, Knopf, 1951), 79–80.

3. Quantification does not necessarily refer to exact counting. It may equally well refer to rough estimates of "more or less," provided only that some relatively stable empirical indices of the value quantified are available, so that estimates can be checked for their validity.

are of primary importance for life and survival. "Everything from the chance to stay alive during the first year after birth to the chance to view fine arts, the chance to remain healthy and grow tall, and if sick to get well again quickly, the chance to avoid becoming a juvenile delinquent—and very crucially, the chance to complete an intermediary or higher educational grade"—all these *life chances* are crucially influenced by one's position in the economic class structure.[4]

The economic structure in turn refers to the amount and source of income:

> Individuals of the same or similar economic position have identical or similar goods and services to offer in the system of production and distribution and therefore receive identical or similar monetary rewards in the market place.[5]

It is, of course, easy to quantify income amounts, and this is the baseline of economic stratification. The source of income is an ambiguous variable, used in conjunction with the first to make predictions (or inferences) about the consumption patterns of individuals and about how they spend their time, and these variables in turn are also subject to measurement. The fact that income *source* is called an economic variable, may, however, produce spurious correlations between the economic and status hierarchies.

There are additional problems in quantification. Some income is received in kind—traditionally in the form of home-grown produce, but more recently in the form of fringe benefits. The availability of tax-supported public services, e.g. public housing, free welfare clinics, and public libraries, also makes a difference in real income. There are, finally, regional differences in purchasing power and various forms of taxation having differential impacts, and they too must be taken into account in order to give a strictly accurate measure of an individual's comparative economic position.[6] However, all of these obstacles can be overcome in principle, and a satisfactory quantification of economic positions can be achieved.

It is an easily defended proposition that wealth, and hence purchasable advantages of various kinds, is unequally distributed in society. That these unequal relations can be ordered transitively seems intuitively ob-

4. Mayer, *Class and Society,* p. 23, quoting Gerth and Mills (*Character and Social Structure*), p. 313.

5. Ibid.

6. Cf. Gideon Sjoberg, "Are Social Classes in America Becoming More Rigid?" *Am. Soc. Rev., 16* (Dec. 1951), 775–83.

vious. It is also obvious that, in normal circumstances, a wife and child enjoy life chances which correspond with those of the head of their household. Finally, wealth, therefore life chances, can pass through inheritance from generation to generation.

Much the same story can be told, with perhaps a few more reservations, of the distribution of social status in society. The social status structure implies that there is a pattern of deference in society in which individuals recognize others as being "above" or "beneath" them, or "on the same level," for purposes of sociability. These inequalities are observed and quantified in a variety of ways: social scientists have recorded numerous sets of self-and-other ratings by individuals in communities, by panels of especially knowledgeable citizens, and by participant observers.[7] Numerous objective criteria are used in the rating process by citizens themselves and by observers. These criteria have included: family background, residence location, occupation, education, social participations (kinds and numbers of social memberships), and "style of life," which subsumes patterns of consumption and adherence to various canons of "taste" and/or "fashion."[8]

Congruence among these various measures of status is not always high, hence instabilities in status are not uncommon.[9] This occasionally prevents a strict transitive status ordering of individuals. A may successfully claim deference from B and B from C in a small town, on account of superiority in family connections. But when they are placed in a metropolitan environment, their consumption patterns may reverse this order or possibly render the exchange of deference entirely unpredictable.

However, the status positions of many families in many communities are apparently relatively well fixed. The fact that this applies to entire families is deemed so well established as to preclude the necessity for empirical testing.[10] In fact, it is generally well known that, while the breadwinner establishes the status of a family, it is his wife who enforces

7. See, for example, Hollingshead, *Elmtown;* Harold F. Kaufman, "Prestige Classes in a New York Rural Community," Cornell Univ. Agricultural Experiment Station, *Memoir 260* (Ithaca, March 1944); W. Lloyd Warner, Marchia Meeker, and Kenneth Eels, *Social Class in America* (Gloucester, Peter Smith, 1957); Gerhard E. Lenski, "American Social Classes: Statistical Strata or Social Groups?" *Am. J. Soc.,* 58 (Sept. 1952), 139–44.

8. See Joseph A. Kahl and James A. Davis, "A Comparison of Indexes of Socioeconomic Status," *Am. Soc. Rev.,* 20 (June 1955), 317–25.

9. See ibid. and Gregory P. Stone and William H. Form, "Instabilities in Status," *Am. Soc. Rev.,* 18 (April 1953), 149–62.

10. However, works such as Hollingshead's *Elmtown* bear out the conclusion that members of different generations in the same nuclear family have similar status positions.

the maintenance of status boundaries and his children who perpetuate these arrangements through their social participations, the most important of which is the marriage market.

All of the foregoing is elementary doctrine of social stratification analysis, to be found in any textbook on the subject.[11] It is mentioned only as an introduction to what should be a surprising observation: that the third famous dimension of stratification analysis, power, fits only one of the criteria of stratification analysis at all well. It is in no wise comparable to the variables class and status in its fit with the criteria of stratification analysis.

Let us consider the first criterion: is it possible for an observer, through empirical observations, to arrive at an estimate of who has more and who has less power? This has never been done in stratification studies except by definition. Thus C. Wright Mills *defines* as America's power elite those occupying specified positions in military, economic, and political hierarchies.[12] Milton Gordon cites power as a dimension of social stratification, owing to the fact that power distributions are "inherently hierarchical." [13] But we must reject the substitution of definition for observation because obviously a construct which exists in language need not exist in the real world, and the task of stratification analysis is to clarify man's social behavior, not to indulge in circularities.

Another attempt to satisfy the first criterion holds that power can be observed empirically, but suggests as evidence the identical observations which were used as indices of economic or status positions. As an example of this, Kurt B. Mayer says in his text:

> We have defined power as the ability to control the behavior of others. Sociologically, power refers especially to the control which certain groups and individuals are able to exercise over the life chances of others.[14]

The difficulty with this formulation is that the "life chances" of an individual refers to the characteristic which defines his *economic* position,

11. E.g. Barber, *Social Stratification*, p. 74; Cuber and Kenkel, *Social Stratification in the U.S.*, pp. 71–73, 176–78; Kahl, *American Class Structure*, pp. 142 ff., 190; Warner, Meeker, and Eels, *Social Class in America*, p. 10; Talcott Parsons, *Essays in Sociological Theory* (rev. ed., Glencoe, Free Press, 1954), p. 422.

12. C. Wright Mills, *The Power Elite* (New York, Oxford Univ. Press, 1956), passim, esp. chap. 1.

13. Gordon, *Social Class in American Sociology*, pp. 238–39, 243 ff. See also Cuber and Kenkel, *Social Stratification in the U.S.*, p. 322.

14. Mayer, *Class and Society*, p. 26.

as we have seen.[15] When one individual controls the life chances of another, this is usually an indication of his superior *economic* position (e.g.
boss vs. employee). Thus "control over the life chances of others" is at
best a highly ambiguous criterion for use as an index of the power of
actors, and, at worst, the observations suggested by this criterion are
identical with those one would make to ascertain the economic class
position or life chances of an individual. Others make an analogous mistake with respect to social status.[16] As long as we adhere to the notion
that power is an empirically separable variable of social stratification,
we must reject these as improper, and search for specific, separate empirical indices by which power can be measured. Stratification analysis
has so far failed to fulfill this criterion.

As for the second criterion, it seems intuitively obvious that power is
distributed unequally in society. But this most basic of criteria merely
invites us to state the shape and durability of the inequality.

The difficulty of making such a statement becomes plain when we
attempt to satisfy the criterion of transitivity. Robert Dahl states the
dilemma nicely:

> With an average probability approaching one, I can induce each
> of 10 students to come to class for an examination on a Friday after-
> noon when they would otherwise prefer to make off for New York
> or Northampton. With its existing resources and techniques, the New
> Haven Police Department can prevent about half the students who
> park along the streets near my office from staying beyond the legal

15. Ibid., p. 23. Neal Gross, arguing from evidence in Mayer's "The Theory of
Social Classes," comes to a similar conclusion. He also confirms my impression that
Mayer's work ably represents the current central tendency in stratification theorizing.
Gross, "A Critique of 'Social Structure and American Educaton,'" *Harvard Educational Review,* 23 (Fall 1953), 298–329. The one significant attempt to overcome
the disabilities of presuming, without a further attempt at empirical confirmation, that
power is an epiphenomenon of class and status position is the so-called "influence
attribution" method used by Floyd Hunter and others. Hunter, *CPS.* But this method
also presumes that power is coextensive with class and status, and thus suffers from
the same methodological handicap as studies which do not use this device. See
especially Raymond E. Wolfinger, "Reputation and Reality in the Study of 'Community
Power,'" *Am. Soc. Rev.,* 25 (Oct. 1960), 636–44; also Dahl, "Critique," 463–69;
Nelson W. Polsby, "Three Problems in the Analysis of Community Power," *Am. Soc.
Rev.,* 24 (Dec. 1959), 795–803.

16. See, for example, Baltzell, *Philadelphia,* pp. 32 ff. Warner, Meeker, and Eels,
Social Class in America, p. 8. David Riesman makes the following pungent comment:
"All the arguments which go on so tiresomely . . . between Warner and the Marxists
seem to me an argument as to which status system runs the country, when, in fact,
neither does"; "Some Observations Concerning Marginality," *Phylon, 12* (June 1951),
117.

time limit. Which of us has the more power? The question is, I believe, incapable of being answered unless we are ready to treat my relationships with my students as in some sense comparable with the relations of the Police Department with another group of students. Otherwise any answer would be arbitrary, because there is no valid way of combining the three variables—scope, number of respondents and change in probabilities—into a single scale.[17]

The question of transitivity merely compounds the comparability problem outlined by Dahl. If there is no satisfying way of comparing A's power with B's, then how much less likely it is that we can arrive at some agreement with respect to all three relationships, A-B, B-C, and A-C!

As for the fourth criterion, Robert Schulze has urged that we regard power exercise as a relationship not merely between persons, but between persons occupying particular positions.[18] Thus Professor Dahl's chances of seeing me in an examination on any hypothetical Friday declined precipitously when I completed his courses. This common-sense formulation of the power relation also reveals that the members of a power-holder's family seldom have anything to do with his power exercise, except insofar as they can influence the power-holder directly. Ellen Dahl's ability to detain one or several Yale students in New Haven should not be confused with the comparatively futile efforts her father might make in the same direction.

There are occasional examples in American history where the power of one member of a family was shared among members of his household. The activities of Mrs. Woodrow Wilson during her husband's sickness in office is perhaps the most striking case in point. But no one is likely to mistake an historical rarity for a social pattern.

The final criterion has to do with the inheritance of power by the children of the powerful. No one will deny that there is a tradition in American politics according to which certain families enter public service; several generations of these families have unquestionably been prominent in positions of power and public trust. One thinks, for example, of the Byrds of Virginia, the Longs of Louisiana, Lodges of Massachusetts, and Frelinghuysens of New Jersey. But additional facts must be kept in mind. These positions of public trust are not inherited as a matter of course, but rather must be achieved by some kind of personal accomplishment

17. Robert A. Dahl, "The Concept of Power," *Behavioral Science*, 2 (July 1957), 206.

18. Schulze "Bifurcation."

even by inheritors of a long family tradition of public service. Family background often provides extremely good opportunities for the sons of political notables to display their talents, but their personal accomplishments are by no means irrelevant to their subsequent rise to positions of power in their own right. This of course does not mean that political leaders from politically prominent families necessarily possess unusual competence at the tasks they perform, since those qualities that may be necessary to achieve public office or political leadership—e.g. popularity —are not always useful in the day-to-day conduct of business. In any event, it should be noted that far from a majority of the powerful are children of the powerful, as can be seen by even a casual census of, let us say, current chief executives of American cities and states. And it is also obvious that only a minority of the offspring of the powerful go on to become politically notable themselves.[19] This provides a vivid contrast with the dimensions of class and status, where, as a matter of course, children inherit the positions of their parents. The passage of power by inheritance alone in modern America, while it is not unheard of, is surely a deviant, not a dominant pattern.

If the argument is persuasive that modern American community life is a relatively inappropriate setting for the application of a stratification analysis, then it follows that those who try to make such an analysis run certain risks. The two characteristic pitfalls are similar to those confronting a man doing a jigsaw puzzle. On the one hand, he must not force pieces into places they do not fit. On the other, he must not have any odd pieces left over when he completes his work. As we have seen,

19. Cf. Donald R. Matthews, *The Social Background of Political Decision-Makers* (Garden City, Doubleday, 1954). This book contains at least five methodological difficulties which sharply limit its usefulness in the present context: first, it depends in part for confirmation of its thesis on the community studies whose findings about power have been questioned in this book and elsewhere. Second, Matthews presents data on the occupational distributions of legislators as compared with gross occupational figures for the total American population, without controlling for the systematic constitutional over-representation of rural areas in legislatures, which ought in turn to produce skews in the occupations of legislators: e.g., over-representation of farmers, under-representation of urban workers. Third, Matthews' data are often skimpier than they appear: e.g., there are several tables showing percentage distributions where N's are fewer than 100 and in one case as low as 2. Fourth, social backgrounds have been found to be insufficient data for predicting policy positions in decision-making. See W. W. Charters, Jr., "Social Class Analysis and the Control of Education," *Harvard Educational Review*, 23 (Fall 1953), 268–83, and C. Arnold Anderson, "The Need for a Functional Theory of Social Class," *Rural Sociology*, 19 (June 1954), 152–60. A final point: Matthews presents no data on the *power* positions of parents of political decision-makers, concentrating instead on *economic* positions. Therefore his data fail to test the hypothesis suggested.

stratification studies of community power have on occasion both forced their data and ignored contrary evidence. But this is understandable, since stratification analysis presumes the existence of stable, significant inequalities. Stratification writers have stated this as a finding, but in reality these inequalities are a *presumption* without which stratification analysis is impossible.

But why was stratification theory employed at all? A hypothesis worth exploring is that stratification theory somehow fits the policy preferences or the personal, emotional needs of researchers. This argument is hard to sustain if for no other reason than that stratification writers have in general eschewed direct expositions of their social and political values. In the three instances in which this has not been the case, however, there has been a disparity of views. C. Wright Mills has indicated his distress at the pattern of dominance he detects in modern society, characterizing it as conducive to a "higher immorality." [20] Digby Baltzell, on the other hand, celebrated the identical pattern in Philadelphia as a necessary check on the abuse of power by leaders unacculturated to upper-class *noblesse oblige*.[21] The Lynds expressed great discontent at the low standards of administrative morality and efficiency which prevailed in Middletown as the result of the alleged withdrawal of the "better" people from political life, but they also decried the antidemocratic hegemony of the business class, thus placing themselves on both sides of the question.[22]

We can say, then, that diametrically opposed policy positions are supported equally well by the stratification analysis of community power. The five key propositions can be deduced from the social values of neither Mills nor Baltzell. Nor can either set of values be deduced from their "findings" about power. It is possible that several researchers were led to the same false conclusion each for a different reason. But I am proceeding on the assumption that this was not the case and that a common source of error exists.

20. Mills, *The Power Elite*, passim, esp. chap. 15. See also Mills, *White Collar* (New York, Oxford Univ. Press, 1953); Mills, "The Power Elite: Comment on Criticism," *Dissent, 4* (Winter 1957), 22–34; Mills, "The Middle Classes in Middle-sized Cities," *Am. Soc. Rev., 11* (Oct. 1946), 520–29; Mills and Melville Ulmer, *Small Business and Civic Welfare: Report of the Smaller War Plants Corporation,* U.S. Senate Document 134, 79th Cong., 2d Sess. (Washington, Government Printing Office, 1946).

21. Baltzell, *Philadelphia*, pp. 4–5, 60–63.

22. See Lynd, *M*, e.g. pp. 414, 425–29 and Lynd, *MIT*, e.g. pp. 123, 322, 364. This point is elaborated in Polsby, "Power in Middletown: Fact and Value in Community Research," *Canadian Journal of Economics and Political Science, 26* (Nov. 1960), 592–603.

If the political views of researchers do not provide a suitable rationale for the employment of stratification theory, one may hypothesize that the intellectual framework of stratification theory was a natural one for sociologists to use. According to one prevailing opinion among sociologists, stratification theory was erroneously supposed by researchers to have been inappropriate for the study of American life until certain twentieth-century events—notably the depression—reawakened interest in the study of social inequality and in the Marxian prophecy of capitalist self-destruction.[23] By the time most of the studies discussed in this book were written, stratification theory was enjoying great popularity, and it is not too much to say that today stratification analysis is one of the commonest, most conventional perspectives from which sociologists view social life.

I turn, finally, to certain basic presumptions, axioms, and definitions of stratification theory itself, for the light they may throw on the source of common error. The first hypothesis suggested reasons why the application of stratification theory might have been expected to produce errors in describing social reality. The present discussion attempts to discover why these particular errors, embodied in the five key propositions, were made.

Stratification means, of course, the division of the community into strata, or layers, one on top of the other. Each individual in the community can in principle be located in a layer, and no one is found in more than a single layer at any point in time. This suggests that by some criterion or other there is always an identifiable top layer in the community, whose members are more or less firmly fixed in place.

Power, in stratification theory, consists of the *capacity* to realize one's will, even over objections.[24] The emphasis upon capacity is important,

23. It is interesting to note that the depression intervened between the writing of the first and the second Middletown books. The second, *Middletown in Transition*, contains by far the more elaborate discussion of power in Middletown and shows a distinct Marxist influence hardly visible in *Middletown*. See also Kingsley Davis, "Introduction" to Kahl, *American Class Structure*, Shils, *Present State of American Sociology*, p. 15; Robert E. L. Faris, "American Sociology" in G. Gurvitch and W. E. Moore, eds., *Twentieth Century Sociology* (New York, Philosophical Library, 1945), pp. 558–59; Gordon, *Social Class in American Sociology*, pp. 8–9; Howard E. Jensen, "Editorial Note," in ibid., pp. viii–ix. Cf. Leonard Reissman, *Class in American Society* (Glencoe, Free Press, 1959), p. 30; Irving Kristol, "The Study of Man: Class and Sociology," *Commentary*, 24 (Oct. 1957), 358–63.

24. This is Max Weber's famous definition. See H. H. Gerth and C. Wright Mills, eds., *From Max Weber, Essays in Sociology* (New York, Oxford Univ. Press, 1946), pp. 180–95. Weber's framework for the study of power as an aspect of stratification is widely accepted among sociologists. See, for example, Mayer, *Class and Society*, p. 18;

because it signifies the stratification writers' attempt to find some relatively unambiguous set of resources which unfailingly index this capacity
successfully (i.e., which predict the outcomes of conflicts). As we saw
earlier, stratification writers customarily fall back on the indices of high
class or status position as indices of power. Given these presumptions,
one might deduce the first proposition: the upper class rules because the
upper class is at the top of the economic and status hierarchy, and
capacity to realize one's will (or to rule or prevail in decision-making)
is indexed by class and status position.

Another characteristic of stratification analysis is to blur the distinction
between values accruing to an individual and those accruing to a group.
This is a serious matter when collective activity is involved; less so when
individuals deal directly with individuals. In the latter case, let us say that
the middle class, with 40 per cent of the nation's population, has $100
million in wealth, while the upper class, with 3 per cent of the population,
has $50 million. We would say, then, that the per capita wealth of the
upper class was greater, but that the collective wealth of the middle class
was greater. In assessing the life chances of an individual, it is clearly
his per capita value position which is relevant, and not the aggregate
value position of all the members of his class.

But in order to maintain the proposition that the upper class rules,
stratification theory must make the assumption that per capita power is
irrelevant. Rather, the power position of a class must be considered a
collective property, and the upper class always must have more of the
total amount of power in the community than any other group.[25] Without this proviso, we could conceive of situations in which all the members of the more numerous lower classes got together and outvoted the
upper class; hence, the upper class would not rule. The fact that this
sometimes happens suggests one limitation on the utility of the assump-

Kaufman, Duncan, Gross, and Sewell, "Problems of Theory and Method," Schulze,
"Bifurcation"; Herbert Goldhamer and Edward Shils, "Types of Power and Status,"
Am. J. Soc., 45 (Sept. 1939), 171–82; Robert Bierstedt, "An Analysis of Social
Power," *Am. Soc. Rev.*, 15 (Dec. 1950), 730–38; Talcott Parsons, "A Revised
Analytical Approach to the Theory of Social Stratification," in Bendix and Lipset,
eds., *Class, Status and Power*, pp. 92–128; Bendix and Lipset, "Introduction" in ibid.,
p. 13; Hans Gerth and C. Wright Mills, review of W. Lloyd Warner and Paul S. Lunt,
The Social Life of a Modern Community, in *Am. Soc. Rev.*, 7 (April 1942), 263–71;
Floyd Hunter, *Top Leadership: U.S.A.* (Chapel Hill, Univ. of North Carolina Press,
1959).

25. As I have said, stratification writers do not make these distinctions clear. However, see Gerth and Mills, *Character and Social Structure*, pp. 328 ff., esp. 339–41;
Gordon, *Social Class*, pp. 240–45; Mayer, *Class and Society*, pp. 5–6.

tion. But a more serious objection may be raised: how can the power of the class a man belongs to be revealed by his individual life chances? The set of logical leaps which by implication establishes the identity of individual and collective value-positions is an unfortunate aspect of stratification theory. Once accomplished, they enable us to observe that political and civic leaders are subordinate to economic and social leaders because the latter group occupies the top, and no matter how numerous or powerful civic leaders become they can never, by the rules of stratification analysis, collectively exceed the power of the upper class.

A single power elite is seen to rule in American community life because stratification theory provides for differentiation only between ranks in a hierarchy; hence those who belong to some group other than the top group are nonrulers, and all those who belong to the top group are rulers.

The interests of a group may be defined as maximizing its long-run share of values. In stratification theory, every group is presumed to be pursuing its own interests. Insofar as a group fails to do so, it is presumed to lack information and organization. The upper class is presumed to be uniquely endowed with information, organization, and all other conceivable means for pursuing rational activity, i.e., maximizing its long-run share of values.[26] Therefore, the conclusion must be that the upper class rules in its own interests.

A final set of stratification theory presumptions has to do with the scarcity of values in society.[27] This means that each class, in maximizing its own long-run share of values, runs up against other classes bent on the same end. Conflict takes place because values demanded exceed values supplied, and this scarcity sets off class conflict. Again, groups other than classes are not seen as conflicting for values because stratification theory differentiates clearly only between classes; other groups, lacking a place in the basic language of stratification analysis, are not unimportant so much as invisible.

The key propositions of the stratification analysis therefore follow from the basic axioms and definitions of stratification theory. It seems highly improbable that propositions different from those given would appear

26. See Kahl, *American Class Structure*, pp. 159–60; Gordon, *Social Class*, pp. 193 ff.; Mayer, *Class and Society*, pp. 24, 61–68.

27. See Seymour M. Lipset, "Political Sociology," in R. K. Merton, L. Broom, and L. S. Cottrell, Jr., eds., *Sociology Today* (New York, Basic Books, 1959), pp. 105–06; Talcott Parsons, "The Distribution of Power in American Society," *World Politics, 10* (Oct. 1957), 139; Robert S. Lynd, "Power in American Society as Resources and Problem," in Arthur Kornhauser, ed., *Problems of Power in American Society* (Detroit, Wayne State Univ. Press, 1957), pp. 9–10.

as findings in stratification studies, given the assumptions that (1) the community is divided horizontally, into ranked layers, with a single layer on top; (2) power is a collective attribute of classes indexed by the per capita economic and status value positions of class members; (3) classes are oriented to the goal of maximizing their long-run share of values; (4) the total supply of values in the community is smaller than the demands of the various classes. Since each of these conditions is postulated, explicitly or implicitly, in stratification theory, it seems legitimate to conclude that the key propositions could have been deduced from basic axioms. This may explain why stratification writers have advanced similar propositions about community power despite the fact that the propositions were not justified by the facts in the communities they studied.

6. How to Study Community Power:
The Pluralist Alternative

In criticizing the stratification approach to the study of community power, I have suggested, among other things, that this approach encourages research designs which generate self-fulfilling prophecies, that it leads to the systematic misreporting of facts and to the formulation of vague, ambiguous, unrealistic, and unprovable assertions about community power. I now want to discuss an alternative method of studying community power which appears to have successfully avoided these undesirable by-products in a number of community studies.

This alternative research strategy can be called the "pluralist" approach. Old, familiar pluralistic presumptions[1] about the nature of American politics seem to have given researchers strategies for the study of community power which are both feasible to execute and comparatively faithful to conditions in the real world.[2] What follows is an attempt to

1. I am well aware that for other purposes the "pluralist" approach can be divided into several schools of thought. However, all variations of pluralist theory contrast effectively with stratification theory. Pluralist presumptions can be found, for example, in the writings of Tocqueville and Madison and in Arthur Bentley, *The Process of Government* (Chicago, Univ. of Chicago Press, 1908); Pendleton Herring, *The Politics of Democracy* (New York, Rinehart, 1940); David B. Truman, *The Governmental Process* (New York, Knopf, 1953); V. O. Key, Jr., *Politics, Parties and Pressure Groups* (New York, Crowell, 1942 and 1959). More formal treatments of propositions contained in many of these works can be found in Anthony Downs, *An Economic Theory of Democracy* (New York, Harper, 1957); David Braybrooke, "Some Steps toward a Formal System of Political Science," a report prepared for the Committee on Political Behavior of the Social Science Research Council, Sept. 1957; James S. Coleman, "An Examination of Arthur F. Bentley's Theory of Government," ibid., July 1957; and Robert A. Dahl, *A Preface to Democratic Theory* (Chicago, Univ. of Chicago Press, 1956).

2. Among the researchers who have found pluralist presumptions about the nature of the political system useful are Robert A. Dahl (see his "The New Haven Community Leadership Study," Working Paper Number One, Dec. 1957, mimeo.; and *Who Governs?*); Harry Scoble ("Yankeetown"); and George Belknap and Norton E. Long (see Long, "The Local Community as an Ecology of Games," *Am. J. Soc., 64* [Nov. 1958], 251–61; Long and Belknap, "A Research Program on Leadership and

explain why this seems to be the case for pluralist studies, but not for stratification studies.

The first and perhaps most basic presupposition of the pluralist approach is that nothing categorical can be assumed about power in any community. It rejects the stratification thesis that *some* group necessarily dominates a community. If anything, there seems to be an unspoken notion among pluralist researchers that at bottom *nobody* dominates in a town, so that their first question to a local informant is likely to be not "Who runs this community?" but rather "Does anyone at all run this community?" It is instructive to examine the range of possible answers to each of these questions. The first query is somewhat like "Have you stopped beating your wife" in that virtually any response short of total unwillingness to answer will supply the researcher with a "power elite" along the lines presupposed by stratification theory.[3] On the other hand, the second question is capable of eliciting a response which *could* lead to the discovery of a power elite (i.e., "Yes"), or any of an infinite number of stable, but nonelitist patterns of decision-making (i.e., "No, but . . . ," "Yes, but . . .") or total fragmentation, or disorganization (i.e., "No").

What sort of question is likely to follow "Who runs the community?" in a questionnaire? Obviously, something like "*How* do the people named in the above response run the community?" This entirely probable pattern of investigation begs the question whether or not those said to rule actually do rule. In the pluralist approach, on the other hand, an attempt is made to study specific outcomes in order to determine who actually prevails in community decision-making. Because the study of actual outcomes requires arduous and expensive field work, outcomes in a few (but for reasons of expense usually only a few) issue-areas are studied closely. More than a single issue-area is always chosen, however, because of the presumption among pluralist researchers that the same pattern of decision-making is highly unlikely to reproduce itself in more than one issue-area. In this expectation, pluralist researchers have seldom been

Decision-making in Metropolitan Areas," [mimeo., New York, Governmental Affairs Institute, Aug. 1956]; Belknap and John H. Bunzel, "The Trade Union in the Political Community," *PROD*, 2 [Sept. 1958], 3–6; Belknap, "A Plan for Research on the Socio-political Dynamics of Metropolitan Areas," presented before a seminar on urban leadership of the Social Science Research Council, New York, Aug. 1957). See also a paper presented to this seminar by Peter H. Rossi, "The Study of Decision-making in the Local Community."

3. See Herbert Kaufman and Victor Jones, "The Mystery of Power," *Public Administration Review, 14* (Summer 1954), 205–12.

disappointed.[4] They recognize, however, the possibility that the same pattern *could* reproduce itself in more than one issue-area. Since actual behavior is observed or reconstructed from documents, witnesses, and so on, it is possible to determine empirically whether or not the same group rules in two or more issue-areas. The presumption that a power elite is unlikely does not, in other words, prevent finding one.

A superficially persuasive objection to this approach might be phrased as follows: "Suppose research in a community discloses different patterns of decision-making in each of three issue-areas. This does not rule out the possibility that all other issue-areas in the community are dominated by a single power elite." How can pluralists meet this objection? First, it is necessary to acknowledge the *possibility* that this is the case. However, pluralists can (and do) protect themselves in part by studying significant issues. In New Haven, for example, Dahl, Wolfinger, and I studied nominations by the two political parties (which determined who held public office), the urban redevelopment program (the largest in the country, measured by past and present outlays per capita), public education (the most costly item in the city's budget), and a campaign to revise the city charter. In Bennington, Scoble studied political nominations and elections, the issue of consolidation of various municipal governments, the formation of a union high school district, and the construction of a new high school building.[5] A Long and Belknap pilot study of a large eastern city embraced the problems of transportation, race relations, traffic, urban redevelopment, and recreation,[6] and Belknap studied the issues of urban redevelopment, transportation, and race relations in the San Francisco Bay area.[7]

None of these issues is trivial, and a case can be made for the proposition that they were in fact the most important issues before these communities during the time the studies were being carried out. What sort of power elite asserts itself in relatively trivial matters, but is inactive or ineffective in the most significant areas of community policy-making?

Stratification theory holds that power elites fail to prevail only on trivial issues.[8] By preselecting issues generally agreed to be significant,

4. Raymond E. Wolfinger, "Reputation and Reality in The Study of 'Community Power,'" *Am. Soc. Rev.*, 25 (Oct. 1960), pp. 636–44, has summarized findings on this point. See also below, chap. 7.

5. "Yankeetown."

6. "A Research Program."

7. "A Plan for Research."

8. See, for example, Roland J. Pellegrin and Charles H. Coates, "Absentee-owned Corporations and Community Power Structure," *Am. J. Soc.*, 61 (March 1956), 413–19; and Lynd, *MIT*, p. 89.

pluralist researchers can test stratification theory without searching end-
lessly in issue-area after issue-area in order to discover some semblance
of a power elite. After all, we cannot reasonably require of researchers
that they validate someone else's preconceived notion of community
power distributions. If the researcher's design is such that any power
distribution has an equal chance of appearing in his result, we may not
properly criticize his result on the ground that it did not conform to
expectations. The burden of proof is clearly on the challenger in such a
case to make good his assertion that power is actually distributed otherwise.[9]

Another presumption of the pluralist approach runs directly counter
to stratification theory's presumption that power distributions are a more
or less permanent aspect of social structure. Pluralists hold that power
may be tied to issues, and issues can be fleeting or persistent, provoking
coalitions among interested groups and citizens ranging in their duration
from momentary to semi-permanent. There is a clear gain in descriptive
accuracy in formulating power distributions so as to take account of the
dimension of time, as pluralists do.[10] For it is easily demonstrated that
coalitions *do* vary in their permanency, and to presume that the set of

9. See Dahl, "Critique."
10. See, for example, Belknap ("A Plan for Research"), who discusses this explicitly. One stratification writer who has attempted to take account of the time factor
is Jerome K. Myers, "Assimilation in the Political Community," *Sociology and Social
Research*, 35 (Jan.–Feb. 1951), 175–82. Myers plots a secular trend which indicates
slow increases in the number of Italians and Italian-descended employed by New
Haven municipal government over a 50-year period ending in 1940. He claims to
have discovered "discrimination" against Italians, because they did not participate in
city government to an extent proportional with their representation in the total population of the city. His conclusion in 1951 was that "the early or quick assimilation
of New Haven Italians in the political system does not seem very probable. . . . All
indications are that political assimilation is inevitable, although it is at least several
generations away." By taking account of shorter-term cyclical movements within the
allegedly "basic" structure, we may be able to explain the delay in the political
assimilation of Italians. As I have mentioned, New Haven Italians were and are
predominantly Republican in local politics. From 1920 to 1940, years in which the
Italians would "normally" have been expected to come into their own as a politically
significant minority group, the city government was in Democratic hands twice as
much as Republican, and this would lead one to expect Italians to be less well represented among office-holders than if this situation were reversed. However, in 1945,
when William Celentano, a Republican of Italian descent, was elected mayor, Italians
entered the top echelons of city government in large numbers. There is, of course, no
sure way of telling what a "normal" rate of absorption into political positions would
be. More or less comparable data indicate that in New Haven Italians were perhaps
a bit swifter in their rise to political leadership than in Providence, Rhode Island. See
Elmer E. Cornwell, Jr., "Party Absorption of Ethnic Groups: The Case of Providence,
Rhode Island," *Social Forces*, 38 (March 1960), 205–10.

coalitions which exists in the community at any given time is a time-lessly stable aspect of social structure is to introduce systematic inaccuracies into one's description of social reality.

Why do pluralists reject the idea that *some* group necessarily dominates every community? The presumption that communities are likely to be less rather than more permanent in their patterns of decision-making is no doubt part of the answer, but another part is an even more fundamental presumption that human behavior is governed in large part by inertia. This notion leads pluralists to look upon overt activity as a more valid indication of involvement in issues than mere reputations for leadership.[11]

Pluralists refuse to regard particular groups as necessarily implicated in decisions when the groups themselves reject such involvement.[12] For pluralists, the imputation of "false class consciousness" suggests that the values of analysts are being imposed arbitrarily on groups in the community. They reject the idea that there is any particular issue or any particular point in the determination of an issue when a group *must* assert itself in order to follow its expressed values. Rather, the pluralist assumes that there are many issues and many points at which group values can be realized. Further, pluralists presume that there are certain costs in taking any action at all. This refers not simply to the possibility of losing, of making political enemies, and so on, but also to the costs in personal time and effort involved in political mobilization, in becoming informed, in lobbying or campaigning, and in taking the trouble to vote.[13]

It is a demonstrated fact that public activity of all kinds is a habit of the middle and upper classes.[14] Vidich and Bensman, in their community study, depicted the life of the lowest-class groups in the community sufficiently well so that the personally functional aspects of withdrawal from the community were revealed.[15] The presumption of inertia permits

11. See the previous critique of Hunter in Chap. 3, and Wolfinger, "Reputation and Reality."

12. See C. Wright Mills, "The Middle Classes in Middle-sized Cities," *Am. Soc. Rev., 11* (Oct. 1946), 520–29, for the stratification theory view.

13. See Downs, *Economic Theory of Democracy*; see also Samuel Stouffer, *Communism, Conformity and Civil Liberties* (Garden City, Doubleday, 1955), pp. 58 ff.

14. Robert E. Lane, *Political Life: How People Get Involved in Politics* (Glencoe, Free Press, 1959), pp. 220–34; Angus Campbell, Gerald Gurin, and Warren E. Miller, *The Voter Decides* (Evanston, Row, Peterson, 1954), pp. 70–75.

15. Arthur J. Vidich and Joseph Bensman, *Small Town in Mass Society* (Princeton, Princeton Univ. Press, 1958), pp. 69–70, 290–91. Studies of social status have been hampered by a similar problem of upper-class-centeredness. See the criticism of Warner on this point by Seymour Martin Lipset and Reinhard Bendix, "Social Status and Social Structure," *British Journal of Sociology, 2* (June 1951), esp. 163 ff.

the researcher to regard the public sector of activity as but one facet of behavior capable of giving people satisfaction and discourages the inappropriate and arbitrary assignment of upper- and middle-class values to all actors in the community.

The presumption of inertia also helps put economic and social notables into perspective. If a man's major life work is banking, the pluralist presumes he will spend his time at the bank, and not in manipulating community decisions. This presumption holds until the banker's activities and participations indicate otherwise. Once again, it is very important to make the point that this assumption is not scientifically equivalent to its opposite. If we presume that the banker is really engaged in running the community, there is practically no way of disproving this notion even if it is totally erroneous. On the other hand, it is easy to spot the banker who really *does* run community affairs when we presume he does not, because his activities will make this fact apparent. In the absence of the requisite activities, we have no grounds for asserting that the banker in fact does run the community.[16]

The pluralist emphasis on the time-bounded nature of coalitions and on the voluntary aspect of political participation leads to a further contrast with stratification theory, since pluralists hold that the "interest group" and the "public" are the social collectives most relevant to the analysis of political processes. In the sociologist's patois, politically important groups would be called phenomena of "collective behavior" rather than of "social structure."[17] Social classes in stratification theory are populations differentially ranked according to economic or status criteria, which embrace the entire community. Everyone in a community is a member of at least one but no more than one class at any given moment, and no one in the community falls outside the system. This is a legitimate heuristic construction; however, it is a mistake to impute to the apparently inescapable fact of class membership any sort of class consciousness. This

16. See Bentley, *Process of Government,* pp. 175–222, and note at p. 202: "If we can get our social life stated in terms of activity and of nothing else, we have not indeed succeeded in measuring it, but we have at least reached a foundation upon which a coherent system of measurements can be built up. . . . We shall cease to be blocked by the intervention of unmeasurable elements, which claim to be themselves the real causes of all that is happening, and which by their spook-like arbitrariness make impossible any progress toward dependable knowledge."

17. Only one sociologist seems to have realized what this implies for the methods and conclusions of political analysis. See Rudolf Heberle, *Social Movements* (New York, Appleton, 1951). The relevant theory is compactly expounded by Herbert Blumer in "Collective Behavior," which appears in Alfred M. Lee, ed., *Principles of Sociology* (New York, Barnes and Noble, 1953), pp. 167–220.

sociologists have long recognized.[18] But they seem less willing to grant that it is equally incorrect to presume that those sharing similar market or status positions are also equidistant from all the bases of political power, or in fact share class interests. American society has never been noted for its interclass warfare, a fact often reported with great surprise in stratification studies of American communities.[19]

Pluralists, who see American society as fractured into a congeries of hundreds of small special interest groups, with incompletely overlapping memberships, widely differing power bases, and a multitude of techniques for exercising influence on decisions salient to them,[20] are not surprised at the low priority Americans give to their class memberships as bases of social action. In the decision-making of fragmented government—and American national, state, and local governments are nothing if not fragmented—the claims of small, intense minorities are usually attended to.[21] Hence it is not only inefficient but usually unnecessary for entire classes to mobilize when the preferences of class members are pressed and often satisfied in piecemeal fashion. The empirical evidence supporting this pluralist doctrine is overwhelming,[22] however stratification theorists may have missed its significance for them; the fragmentation of American governmental decision-making and of American society makes class consciousness inefficient and, in most cases, makes the political interests of members of the same class different.

Pluralist research is not interested in ascertaining an actor's ranking in a system presumed to operate hierarchically. Rather, pluralists want to find out about leadership *roles*, which are presumed to be diverse and fluid, both within a single issue-area over time and between issue-areas. Long and Belknap, for example, identify the following leadership roles

18. Indeed, Max Weber, the most important founding father of modern stratification analysis, makes just this point. See Weber's "Class, Status, Party," in H. H. Gerth and C. W. Mills, ed., *From Max Weber: Essays in Sociology* (New York, Oxford Univ. Press, 1946), pp. 180–95, esp. p. 184.

19. See, for example, Lynd, *MIT*, pp. 454–55, 509; Alfred Winslow Jones, *Life, Liberty and Property* (Philadelphia, Lippincott, 1941), pp. 336–54; Warner, *Jonesville*, p. 27; C. Wright Mills, "The Middle Classes." Cf. also Richard Centers, *The Psychology of Social Classes* (Princeton, Princeton Univ. Press, 1949), and note the extent to which his conclusions outrun his data.

20. See, for example, Truman, passim; Alexis de Tocqueville, *Democracy in America* (New York, Vintage, 1952), esp. *1:* 181–205, 281–342; *2:* 114–35.

21. See Dahl, *Preface to Democratic Theory.*

22. Truman (*Governmental Process*) summarizes a tremendous amount of this material. For a recent treatment of the same theme in a case study, see Aaron B. Wildavsky, *Dixon-Yates: A Study in Power Politics* (New Haven, Yale Univ. Press, 1962).

in community decision-making: initiation, staffing and planning, communication and publicity, intra-elite organizing, financing, and public sanctioning.[23]

By describing and specifying leadership roles in concrete situations, pluralists are in a position to determine the extent to which a power structure exists. High degrees of overlap in decision-making personnel among issue-areas, or high degrees of institutionalization in the bases of power in specified issue-areas, or high degrees of regularity in the procedures of decision-making—any one of these situations, if found to exist, could conceivably justify an empirical conclusion that some kind of power structure exists. By specifying leadership roles and activities, the pluralist research strategy makes possible an empirical determination and description of the bounds and durability of a community power structure—if there is one, and the stratification theory presumption that community power is necessarily general and relatively immutable can be discarded as arbitrary.

The final contrast I want to make between the pluralist and stratification methods has to do with their differing conceptions of what is meant by "power." As we have seen, stratification theorists emphasize the cataloguing of power bases, or resources available to actors for the exercise of power.[24] Pluralists, on the other hand, concentrate on power exercise itself. This leads to two subsidiary discoveries. First, there are a great many different kinds of resources which can be put to use in the process of community decision-making—many more resources, in fact, than stratification theorists customarily take into account. One list, for example, might include:

1. Money and credit
2. Control over jobs
3. Control over the information of others
4. Social standing
5. Knowledge and expertness
6. Popularity, esteem, charisma
7. Legality, constitutionality, officiality, legitimacy
8. Ethnic solidarity

23. Long and Belknap, "A Research Program," 9–11; See Polsby, "The Sociology of Community Power: A Reassessment," *Social Forces*, 37 (March 1959), 232–36; and Edward C. Banfield, "The Concept 'Leadership' in Community Research," delivered at the meetings of the American Political Science Association, 1958, for similar lists.

24. See above, Chap. 5.

9. The right to vote
10. Time
11. Personal (human) energy[25]

Secondly, resources can be employed with greater or less skill. The elaboration of the ways in which resources are employed enables the pluralist researcher to pay attention to what practical politicians customarily see as the heart of their own craft: the processes of bargaining, negotiation, salesmanship and brokerage, and of leadership in mobilizing resources of all kinds. It is also possible using this approach to make a more realistic evaluation of the actual disposable resources of actors. A corporation may be worth millions, but its policies and liquidity position may be such that it cannot possibly bring these millions into play to influence the outcome of a community decision—even one in which the corporation is vitally interested. And interest itself, as noted above, is differentially distributed in a pattern which pluralists assume is rational for most actors most of the time. For example, Long and Belknap observe:

> Just as business organizations may be disinterested in community affairs because of the national scope of [their] operations, individual businessmen who move or are shifted from city to city may have little opportunity or incentive to participate in community affairs. Some businesses have strong pressures on them to give attention to community and metropolitan problems. Large department stores are particularly tied up with the destiny of the city and must decide whether to keep to the central city or decentralize in suburban shopping centers. Businessmen with a "metropolitan view" would thus be expected to be found here rather than in the branch office of a national corporation.[26]

What are the practical recommendations which emerge from this comparison of stratification and pluralist approaches to the study of community power? [27] First, the researcher should pick issue-areas as the focus of his study of community power. Secondly, he should be able to defend

25. See Robert A. Dahl, "The Analysis of Influence in Local Communities" (mimeo., May 1959), 10; Dahl, "Leadership in a Fragmented Political System: Notes for a Theory," presented to the Social Science Research Council Conference on Metropolitan Leadership, Evanston, Ill., April 1–3, 1960, p. 7.

26. Long and Belknap, "A Research Program," 13–14. This corresponds to the findings—but not the interpretations—of Robert O. Schulze, "The Role of Economic Dominants in Community Power Structure," Am. Soc. Rev., 23 (Feb. 1958), 3–9.

27. This presumes that the researcher wants to make some generalization about the "normal" distributions of power in community decision-making.

these issue-areas as very important in the life of the community. Thirdly, he should study actual behavior, either at first hand or by reconstructing behavior from documents, informants, newspapers, and other appropriate sources. There is no harm in starting with a list of people whose behavior the researcher wishes to study vis-à-vis an issue-area. The harm comes, rather, in attributing some mystic significance to the list, so that the examination of activity and of actual participation in decision-making becomes superfluous. This recommendation is not meant to discourage the researcher from collecting information about the reputations of actors, or their intentions with respect to community issues, or their evaluations about the meanings of community incidents. All of these kinds of data are of immeasurable value in tracing patterns of decision-making. However, they must be accompanied by information about behavior so that the researcher has some way of distinguishing between myths and facts.

The final recommendation is of the same order: researchers should study the outcomes of actual decisions within the community. It is important, but insufficient, to know what leaders want to do, intend to do, and think they can do. The researcher still has to decide on the basis of his own examination of the facts what the actual upshot is of these various intentions, and not conclude prematurely that intentions plus resources inflexibly predetermine outcomes.

7. Notes for a Theory of Community Power

In suggesting that the pluralist approach to the study of community power avoids mistakes which can seriously damage the results of research, I do not mean to imply that a pluralist theory has emerged which successfully explains the shaping and sharing of values in American local life. In fact pluralist writers have thus far attempted only tentatively to construct a theory of community power and decision-making. Yet theory is necessary if substantial progress in the state of knowledge is to take place.[1] Its desirability is not lessened by the fact that it can be converted

1. At least two substitutes for theory are in common use among pluralist researchers who study community power and politics. One substitute is the case method, which focuses research attention upon those features of political life that seem dramaturgically most compelling, or most historically accidental, or unique, or employ some other, similar criterion of reportorial selection. Examples of excellent case studies of decision-making in local communities are: Herbert Kaufman, "Gotham in the Air Age" in Harold Stein, ed., *Public Administration and Policy Development* (New York, Harcourt, Brace, 1952), pp. 143–97; Herbert Kaufman, *The New York City Health Centers*, Inter-University Case Program (University, Ala., Univ. of Alabama Press, 1959); William K. Muir, Jr., *Defending "The Hill" Against Metal Houses*, Inter-University Case Program (University, Ala., Univ. of Alabama Press, 1958); Louis Menand, III, *Hanover Builds a High School*, Inter-University Case Program (University, Ala., Univ. of Alabama Press, 1959). See also Martin Myerson and Edward Banfield, *Politics, Planning and the Public Interest* (Glencoe, Free Press, 1955); Peter B. Clark, *The Chicago Big Businessman as a Civic Leader* (mimeo., New Haven, Sept. 1959); James Q. Wilson, "Negro Leaders in Chicago" (unpub. doctoral dissertation, Univ. of Chicago, Aug. 1959). A second substitute for theory is the use of metaphors, such as those which currently describe the local community as an "ecology of games" or a "contest for prizes." See Norton E. Long, "The Local Community as an Ecology of Games," *Am. J. Soc.*, 64 (Nov. 1958), 251–61; Herbert Kaufman, "Metropolitan Leadership: The Snark of the Social Sciences," presented to the Social Science Research Council Conference on Metropolitan Leadership, Evanston, Ill., April 1–3, 1960. See also Wallace S. Sayre and Herbert Kaufman, *Governing New York City* (New York, Russell Sage, 1960). Neither of these substitutes for theory systematically misguides research as stratification theory apparently does. The major criticism to be leveled against these devices is that they do not go far enough in organizing data. (Cf. Anatol Rapoport, "Various Meanings of 'Theory,'" *Am. Pol. Sci. Rev.*, 52 [Dec. 1958], 972–88). Case studies leave to their readers the task of determining how findings add to previous knowledge. When findings are not explicitly stated so that they relate to previous information, they may be lost altogether. This, on the whole, seems more wasteful than if case writers were to advance general propositions which accurately reflected their admittedly limited data, even if ultimately they proved to

by the unwary into ideology, thus imprisoning rather than disciplining thought.

If a theory of community power were to exist, what would it tell us? It might, perhaps, tell us who rules, and what the conditions are of rulership. In the first chapter, I suggested that the question "who rules?" could be broken into three component parts, allowing us to speak of three characteristic problems which a theory of community power might help to solve: (1) the problem of identifying and characterizing participants in decision-making, (2) the problem of determining who gains and who loses from outcomes of decisions, (3) the problem of discovering what makes for successful participation in decision-making.[2]

WHO PARTICIPATES?

One of the most common patterns of behavior to be observed in American community life is that participation in the making of decisions is concentrated in the hands of a few. But this does not mean that Amer-

be wrong most of the time. A hypothesis (which sets forth conditions and consequences) even though incorrect is easier to relate to new experience than are collections of unexceptionable, but unorganized anecdotes. See the similar comments by Kaufman in "The Next Step in Case Studies," *Public Administration Review, 18* (Winter 1958), 52–59. Metaphors have the advantage of sensitizing readers and researchers to certain orders of data, but provide little information about the conditions necessary for their proper application. The circumstances under which a community is not an ecology of games or a contest for prizes are worth knowing. We also would like to know when one or another kind of ecology or contest is held to exist; but directions on how to use the metaphor are not given on the package. One illustration of the ease with which these metaphors can be applied to almost any situation has already cropped up in the literature. Klapp and Padgett discovered, by methods apparently similar to those employed by Delbert C. Miller, that there was a "power elite" in Tiajuana, Mexico, but that this "group" did not interact frequently nor did it have much to do with community decision-making or political activity. Klapp and Padgett decided that the "pyramid" metaphor originally sponsored by Hunter could not be used. They also rejected Miller's "concentric ring" image, for reasons not entirely clear to me. Instead, Tiajuana was labeled an "ecology of games" because, apparently, "Tiajuana has no government." Orrin E. Klapp and L. Vincent Padgett, "Power Structure and Decision-making in a Mexican Border City," *Am. J. Soc., 65* (Jan. 1960), 400–06. If the application of the metaphor to these confusing findings represents a gain in knowledge, it is not clear just what this gain might be. The widespread use of metaphors may have the deleterious effect of persuading researchers who employ them that they have something more than a case study with a label on it. But until the labels are so formulated as to discriminate among case studies, we may in fact have something less.

2. For alternative programmatic statements, see H. Douglas Price, "Research on Metropolitanism: Economics, Welfare and Politics" (mimeo., Columbia Univ., Summer 1959); and Peter H. Rossi, "A Theory of Community Structure," delivered at the annual meeting of the American Sociological Society, Chicago, Sept. 1959.

ican communities are ruled by a single all-purpose elite, after the fashion suggested by stratification theory. At least three significant modifications to the finding of limited participation in decision-making must be made. First, different small groups normally make decisions on different community problems, and, likewise, the personnel of decision-making groups often change, even over the short run.[3] Secondly, the decisions made by small groups are almost always considered routine or otherwise insignificant by most other members of the community. Thirdly, when small groups undertake innovation or decision-making in cases salient or likely to become salient to others in the community they must achieve special kinds of legitimacy or risk the likelihood of failure.

The finding that participants in decision-making are largely specialized to certain issue-areas has been confirmed by data gathered using both the methods prevalent in community power research. When citizens or "experts" were asked to nominate leaders in specific issue-areas (as against a more general "who's got the power around here" question employed by Hunter, Miller, and others), different leaders emerged in different issue-areas.

For example, Smuckler and Belknap report in a study of "Community A," Michigan,[4] that, despite severe limitations imposed by the influence attribution method, respondents indicated that most leaders tended to concentrate their efforts in one of a few issue-areas. Unfortunately, the population quizzed about leadership in specific issue-areas was quite restricted, and several of the issue-areas discussed were interrelated in community action programs, thus artificially muting the effects of issue-specialization in the community. Still, Smuckler and Belknap found that while there was a group of top leaders named which overlapped in several local issues,[5] different top leaders within the community were named as influential in local, state, and national affairs, people nominated as leaders in school problems were held to be inactive in community devel-

3. For evidence on this last point, see Donald Olmsted, "Organizational Leadership and Social Structure in a Small City," *Am. Soc. Rev.*, 19 (June 1954), 275–81.

4. Ralph H. Smuckler and George M. Belknap, *Leadership and Participation in Urban Political Affairs* (East Lansing, Governmental Research Bureau, Michigan State Univ., 1956), and Belknap and Smuckler, "Political Power Relations in a Mid-west City," *Public Opinion Quarterly*, 20 (Spring 1956).

5. As well as being quizzed on leadership on specific issues, respondents were also asked to name the "most important people in town when it comes to making decisions about local public affairs here in Community A." This produced a top general elite of 15 names upon whom a relatively large number of respondents were agreed. For reasons given in Chapter 3, I regard this question as misleading, so my summary of findings in Community A emphasizes responses given to more specific questions.

opment programs, and, finally, different top leaders were nominated by different groups in the population.

Scoble's findings in Yankeetown are similar.[6] Out of 69 individuals who were nominated as leaders, roughly half were confined to a single issue-area. Of 27 "general leaders," only 4 were considered influential in the three issue-areas Scoble studied; 9 were named in two policy areas, 9 in only one, and 5 in *none* of the areas Scoble studied.[7] Scoble attempted to test the agreement of the influence attribution method with observed behavior by constructing an "index of leadership activity," which correlated rather poorly with leadership nomination.[8] Scoble indicates that high public visibility and office-holding rather than actual leadership activity is associated with "general leadership" nominations.[9] In fact, in the two community controversies he studied, Scoble concluded that "different sets of leaders were activated . . . however similar the controversies seem."[10]

In an early study of influence attributions which did not take up questions relating to community decision-making, Merton reports that influentials in the town of Revere were specialized in their preoccupations and orientations, either to matters of strictly local concern or to national and international events.[11] "Locals" tended to hold political posts "ordinarily obtained through political and personal relationships." "Cosmopolitans," on the other hand, more often appeared in public positions involving the utilization of special skills and knowledge, e.g. on the Board of Health or the Board of Education. Respondents to Merton's survey tended to name as influential people close to themselves in overall amount of influence. Although interpersonal influence was reported to be concentrated among a relatively few individuals, the bulk of all influence exerted in the community was dispersed among a large number of relatively uninfluential persons. Finally, Merton suggests that the number of topics upon which a citizen was influential varied considerably from person to person.

Agger and Ostrom found that two out of three leaders held to be generally most influential by the population of a small Oregon village were actually restricted in their concerns: one to welfare policies, the other to "seeking the amelioration of specific conditions in his [lower-class] con-

6. "Yankeetown." 8. Ibid., 18.
7. Ibid., 12–13. 9. Ibid., 26–27.
10. Ibid., 38.
11. Robert K. Merton, "Patterns of Influence," in Paul F. Lazarsfeld and Frank N. Stanton, eds., *Communications Research, 1948–1949* (New York, Harper, 1949), pp. 180–219.

stituency."[12] This top trio was associated in a card-playing group with a few other men whose roles are characterized as "more specialized in terms of both their arena of activity and the function they performed." [13] Agger, presenting figures on leadership nominations, indicates that among seven top leaders named as "generally" most influential in the community, *all* were specialized to local government matters, school matters, or community welfare. An eighth top leader was named by nobody as generally influential, but he received 47 per cent of all nominations as most influential in community welfare problems. Only one of the top eight leaders received more than a few nominations in more than one issue-area. Twenty-eight out of thirty-four "advisors" in the community told Agger that they were asked for advice in only one issue-area.[14]

Agger and Ostrom conclude that "participation in policy-making at the local level tends to be specialized for most people in terms of the types of policies with which they concern themselves and in terms of the policy-making arena in which they act." [15]

Fanelli reports similar findings in his study of "Bakerville," Mississippi, where leaders were thought to be specialized to issue-areas on account of their occupations.[16] Leaders were rated both by respondents in the general population and by fellow-nominees according to their general and special influence, and by fellow-nominees alone according to their interactions on community issues. Fanelli suggests that leaders play different kinds of roles within issue-areas; some are considerably more active than others who are rated equally influential by the general population.

The same general finding of specialization of elites was also made by students who used research techniques more closely approximating the "total immersion" approach employed in New Haven. McKee, for example, reports that leadership in Lorain, Ohio, was divided in many ways.[17] "There is no single locus of decision-making, but rather a number

12. Robert E. Agger and Vincent Ostrom, "The Political Structure of a Small Community," *Public Opinion Quarterly*, 20 (Spring 1956), 84.

13. Robert E. Agger and Vincent Ostrom, "Political Participation in a Small Community" in H. Eulau, S. Eldersveld, and M. Janowitz, eds., *Political Behavior* (Glencoe, Free Press, 1956), p. 141.

14. Robert E. Agger, "Power Attributions in the Local Community," *Social Forces*, 34 (May 1956), 325–26.

15. Agger and Ostrom, "Political Participation," p. 140.

16. A. Alexander Fanelli, "A Typology of Community Leadership Based on Influence and Interaction within the Leader Sub-system," *Social Forces*, 34 (May 1956), 332–38.

17. James B. McKee, "Status and Power in the Industrial Community: A Comment on Drucker's Thesis," *Am. J. Soc.*, 58 (Jan. 1953), 364–70. For other more fragmentary, but generally corroborative, reports of industrial communities, see C. W. M.

of loci, each differently structured. Within the corporation is one, within the community are several, and there are other significant ones within the larger society." In Lorain, a single steel mill provided more than half the local jobs, making it a company town in many ways. Collective bargaining was not carried on in the local community, but in Pittsburgh. However this does not mean that the local union was weak. On the contrary, deprived of this central sphere of activity, union leaders moved into local politics and defeated an upper-class Republican coalition which had maintained itself by exploiting ethnic divisions among working-class voters.

The union was also instrumental in "wresting control of the educational system from the upper stratum. However . . . in contrast to municipal politics, the individuals who have sought leadership here . . . have been distinguished . . . on the basis of their policy toward the functioning of the school system." Finally, in the area of civic welfare, the upper stratum remained largely in control, but this control was legitimized by the presence on the requisite boards of directors of a small minority of union leaders who used these memberships not to influence welfare policy but to gain civic respectability for themselves and their union.

The pattern of decision-making by small minorities, largely specialized within issue-areas, is also reported by the Lynds in Middletown, as we have seen. This pattern apparently holds for New Haven and, as Sayre and Kaufman observe, for New York City as well. As Kaufman says:

> Decisions of the municipal government emanate from no single source, but from many centers; conflicts and clashes are referred to no single authority, but are settled at many levels and at many points in the system: no single group can guarantee the success of any proposal it supports, the defeat of every idea it objects to. Not even the central governmental organs of the city—the Mayor, the Board of Estimate, the Council—individually or in combination, even approach mastery in this sense.
>
> Each separate decision center consists of a cluster of interested contestants, with a "core group" in the middle, invested by the rules with the formal authority to legitimize decisions (that is to promul-

Hart, "Industrial Relations Research and Social Theory," *Canadian Journal of Economics and Political Science*, 15 (Feb. 1949), 53–73; Charles R. Walker, *Steeltown* (New York, Harper, 1950); Alfred Winslow Jones, *Life, Liberty and Property* (Philadelphia, Lippincott, 1941); Joel Seidman, Jack London, and Bernard Karsh, "Political Consciousness in Local Unions," *Public Opinion Quarterly*, 15 (Winter 1951–52), 692–702.

gate them in binding form) and a constellation of related "satellite groups" seeking to influence the authoritative issuances of the core group.[18]

Specialization of leadership within issue-areas is one important pattern of participation which modifies the stratification analysis picture of rule by small numbers of people. Another important pattern which modifies and constrains the rule of the few has to do with the grant of legitimacy made to these small groups, entitling them to make decisions. Careful examination of the evidence at hand seems to indicate that elites are freest in their power to commit the resources of the community when decisions are relatively routine and innocuous; other kinds of decision-making—of a nonroutine, unbureaucratized, or innovative variety—seems to require special consent by citizens who fall outside the small decision-making group.

If this pattern is correctly identified, certain propositions can be seen to follow from it. We might reasonably expect, for example, (1) that a general elite, where one is found to exist, would place great emphasis upon maintenance of sociability and contact with a wide range of citizens in the community and less emphasis upon accomplishment, "doing things," or innovation; that in fact these general elites would seek to restrict their own activities in various ways; (2) that elite groups which wanted to innovate would seek systematically to acquire consent from nonelite members of the community; (3) that attempts by elites to put programs into effect without achieving wider legitimacy in the community would fail; and (4) that nonelite members of the community would seek to bring elites under control in areas of concern to them.

The evidence which has begun to accumulate on each of these points indicates that they are true, and hence we can say that in a wide range of community situations participation in decision-making is limited to a relatively few members of the community, but only by the easily revoked consent of a much larger percentage of the local population.[19]

On the propensity of general elites to be self-limiting in their influence, we have the testimony of Scoble, Vidich and Bensman, and Merton, who

18. Kaufman, "Metropolitan Leadership," p. 5. More fully in Sayre and Kaufman, *Governing New York City*, pp. 710 ff.

19. Of course most political issues are entirely uninteresting to most people. Thus, the "larger percentage" I speak of here should not be interpreted as meaning "a majority," except in unusual circumstances. See Samuel Stouffer, *Communism, Conformity and Civil Liberties* (Garden City, Doubleday, 1955), pp. 58–69; and e.g. Raymond Bauer, Ithiel Pool, and Lewis A. Dexter, *American Business and Public Policy* (Atherton, New York, 1963).

speaks of their preoccupation with sociability rather than achievement.[20] Scoble points out that the "general leaders" of Yankeetown seemed to be able to reach the greatest amount of agreement among themselves on the least important issues but were split and competed with one another for the support of nonleaders on issues that were salient to "publics" in the community.[21] Even more striking than self-limitation by competition was the self-limitation by abdication which general leaders imposed upon themselves in "Springdale," where Vidich and Bensman report greater agreement among these leaders on the contents of public policy than seems to have been the case in Yankeetown. But about the exercise of power based on this agreement, Vidich and Bensman say:

> at almost every point in [their] seemingly broad . . . political do-
> main the village and town boards adjust their action to either the
> regulations and laws defined by state and federal agencies which
> claim parallel functions on a statewide or nationwide basis or to the
> fact that outside agencies have the power to withhold subsides to
> local political institutions. . . . The village board in Springdale ac-
> cepts few of the powers given to it. . . . Town and village govern-
> ments find it hard to act even when they have the power.[22]

Evidence gathered in New Haven, especially on the redevelopment is-
sue, indicates the extent to which successful innovation depended upon the broadly based community consensus which was systematically built and nurtured by the mayor. When this sort of consensus is not sought or achieved, failure is not uncommon, as in the New Haven charter reform battle, and as Schulze demonstrates in recounting the painful lesson learned by the proponents of the new Cibola city charter, who had neglected to seek the consent of representatives of laboring and Negro groups.[23] Paul Miller cites figures which indicate that community at-
tempts to build new hospitals were much more successful when they had the backing of local government leaders than when they were carried out strictly under private auspices.[24] As Ross and others have pointed out, private and semi-public charitable organizations and money-raising cam-

20. Merton, "Patterns of Influence."

21. Scoble, "Yankeetown," p. 39.

22. Arthur J. Vidich and Joseph Bensman, *Small Town in Mass Society* (Princeton, Princeton Univ. Press, 1958), pp. 98–100.

23. On New Haven charter reform, see Raymond E. Wolfinger, *The Politics of Progress* to be published by Yale University Press, and Dahl, *Who Governs?* pp. 264–67. On Cibola charter reform, see Schulze, "Bifurcation."

24. Paul A. Miller, "The Process of Decision-making within the Context of Community Organization," *Rural Sociology, 17* (June 1952), 153–61.

paigns are generally controlled by the wealthy, so it is easy to deduce
that one significant difference between public and private auspices in hos-
pital fund-raising is the extent to which members of all segments of the
community are allowed to participate.[25]

We can interpret the failure of elite-backed community programs from
lack of popular support—either in votes or money—as one device through
which members of nonelites seek to bring elites under control. Warner's
data suggests that the unionization of the mills in Yankee City was an
example of another such device, namely the promotion of counterelites.[26]
A third device for bringing elites under control and enlarging the extent
of community participation in decision-making is, as Coleman has indicated, the promulgation of controversy and conflict.[27]

Coleman has summarized numerous instances in which innovation by
elites in community affairs was prevented because they lacked special
grants of legitimacy. A typical pattern of community conflict identified
by Coleman occurs when community leaders have failed to respond
sympathetically to seemingly minor complaints by small groups of citizens. "Little" instances of administrative arbitrariness occasionally draw
sympathy to the victims from other citizens who have quite different axes
to grind; and the resulting public commiseration may lead to widespread
and serious attacks on the legitimacy of many or all administrative activities. Coleman's work suggests the hypothesis that the more people become attentive to community policy-making, the more likely it is that
anti-administration outcomes will ensue.

Striking evidence for this proposition is contained in a tabulation showing all available results of community referenda on the installation of
fluoridation equipment (initiated by city administrations) between November 1951 and November 1955 in the United States.[28] The table suggests that most citizens are drawn into political participation when they
have an objection to register, rather than when they have been sold on a
political program they want to support. It also indicates that those who
are only occasionally involved in community affairs prevail more often
than not over those who are inclined to be regular in their participation,

25. Aileen D. Ross, "The Social Control of Philanthropy," *Am. J. Soc.*, 58 (March
1953), 451–60; Ross, "Philanthropic Activity and the Business Career," *Social Forces*,
32 (March 1954), 274–80; Ross, "Control and Leadership in Women's Groups: An
Analysis of Philanthropic Money-raising Activity," *Social Forces*, 37 (Dec. 1958),
124–31; McKee, "Status and Power"; Lynd, *MIT*, pp. 79, 139, 140.

26. See Warner, YC 4, passim.

27. James S. Coleman, *Community Conflict* (Glencoe, Free Press, 1957).

28. Ibid., p. 19.

TURNOUT

	Under 10%	Over 30%
Fluoridation won	58%	37%
lost	42%	63%
	100%	100%
Number of cases	19	38

when those who are less involved turn out. But note that decision-makers even in a conflict situation and for a referendum still typically are less than a majority of the population. "High" turnout in Coleman's table means "Over 30%." [29]

Another area of interest concerns the paths people travel in order to become involved in decision-making. Information concerning leadership recruitment is fragmentary in many community studies, but enough information exists for us to infer that few if any authoritative community decision-making groups are made up of participants whose backgrounds are entirely homogeneous. Contrary to the stratification theory assumption that leadership recruitment is a process whereby top leaders pull into their midst congenial new blood, there is a good deal of evidence that decision-makers become so by *self-selection*—pushing themselves into the leadership group by showing interest, willingness to work, and competence.[30]

29. The table also underscores the relative rarity of the New Haven experience, where the mayor sought to achieve special legitimacy for his redevelopment program and succeeded for a time in increasing both turnout in mayoralty elections *and* his margin of victory.

30. This was evidently the dominant pattern in New Haven (see above, Chap. 4; Dahl, *Who Governs?*; and Wolfinger's forthcoming *Politics of Progress*); in urban renewal on the south side of Chicago (see Peter H. Rossi and Robert A. Dentler, *The Politics of Urban Renewal* [New York, Free Press of Glencoe, 1961]); in Lorain (see McKee, "Status and Power"); in Yankeetown (see Scoble); and in New York City (see Sayre and Kaufman, *Governing New York City*). One supposes that in each community a minimal amount of resources of some kind are necessary for participation in decision-making to be possible, but this minimum must vary tremendously from issue to issue and depend less upon sheer amount than upon the skill and dedication with which resources are manipulated. Clark (*Chicago Big Businessman*) describes most Chicago big businessmen as relatively ineffective in community decision-making, and Wilson ("Negro Leaders in Chicago") paints a similarly pessimistic picture of leadership in the Chicago Negro community. Yet Rossi and Dentler report that the single actor who succeeded most consistently in getting what he wanted from South Side Chicago urban renewal was an unprepossessing Negro dining-car waiter named Victor Towns, who was not even a leader or high in status in the Negro community. He was, however, extremely diligent in pressing claims on renewal planners in behalf of the welfare of his block, which he legitimately represented. The

Presumably, a theory of community power would attempt to specify the conditions under which different patterns of participation—that is to say, of specialization, legitimacy, recruitment, and reciprocal controls between elites and nonelites—exist. A second major task for such a theory is the examination of the distribution of values in decision-making, which carries us into a discussion of the nature of community decisions.

WHO GAINS, WHO LOSES?

If politics is who *gets* what, when, and how, then knowing who appears to receive indulgences and who appears to suffer deprivations from community decisions should presumably be helpful in identifying possessors of community power. Let us keep two different indices separate for the moment: simply *getting* things that are generally valued is the matter at hand; getting what one *wants* or *prefers* is quite another and will be discussed later. I am going to suggest reasons why knowing value distributions is insufficient and perhaps misleading in discovering who rules. Briefly, these reasons are: (1) value distributions occur without explicit decisions taking place, hence may tell us nothing about decision-making; (2) values within the community may be distributed in important ways as a by-product of decisions and nondecisions made outside the community; (3) there are many irrationalities in decision-making, which may lead to the distribution of values in unpredictable, unintended ways; (4) the powerful may intentionally distribute values to the nonpowerful.

We commonly speak of decisions as "choices among alternatives," [31] and immediately it becomes necessary to clarify the notion of "choice" when used to describe collective decision-making. It is easy enough (though, as I shall suggest below, misleading) to postulate an individual, or a small group of individuals, consciously considering an array of possible future events, consulting their list of goals, and picking a course of action which they calculate will lead to the most preferred state of affairs. This is in fact more or less the process advanced by stratification writers as descriptive of community decision-making. But the evidence indicates that decentralized, fragmented, constrained, reversible, and relatively uncoordinated (as among issue-areas) decision-making is the rule. This leads to the possibility that many outcomes, seen from the per-

---

possession of certain kinds of resources may, in fact, render leaders vulnerable to pressure, as in the case of prosperous retail businessmen who nonetheless remain dependent upon local good will. See Kenneth Wilson Underwood, *Protestant and Catholic* (Boston, Beacon, 1957).

31. See, e.g., Herbert A. Simon, *Administrative Behavior* (2d ed. New York, Macmillan, 1957), pp. 3–4.

spective of the entire community, are not intended by anybody, and consequently who "wins" indulgences in these cases cannot be construed as indicative of the *power* of actors, though it may correctly indicate some other of their value-positions.

Norton Long gives the example of a community which every day is collectively fed, clothed, employed, and sheltered, not as the result of a single program, but rather by the individual activities of myriad citizens, none of whom intend, or are concerned with, the collective outcome. [32] There is at least one sense, then, in which many payoffs of community life must be considered fortuitous and beyond the control of actors in the system.

A second instance in which this may be true is when the community is affected by forces from outside. National and international events of all kinds have their repercussions in community life: war industry in neighboring communities provoked the outmigration of the Morris, Illinois, labor force; the depression accentuated the dependence of Muncie upon the largesse of the Ball family; the war stopped school construction in New Haven, and postponed until 1945 the emergence of an Italian candidate for mayor, who rode to power on the school issue; the Federal Housing Act of 1949 provided essential resources for Mayor Lee's urban renewal venture. The list can be extended indefinitely. At most, actors within the community can take into account these larger forces in making their private calculations; they can only rarely alter the impact these events have on the life of the community. [33]

We can say, then, that many community "decisions" are unconscious, intended by nobody in the community, and yet have profound consequences for the shaping and sharing of community values. Let us move next to the consideration of *conscious* decisions, where choices are made by actors from a set of more or less explicitly delineated alternatives. The way in which this array is conceived is critical. Some, perhaps most, *possible* courses of action are never considered in community decision-making simply because they are inconceivable to the actors involved. No one seems ever to have seriously considered turning the privately owned New Haven Water Company over to the city, for example, although there seems to be no reason why this could not be done. The array of alterna-

32. Long, "Local Community as an Ecology of Games," p. 251.

33. See Vidich and Bensman, *Small Town in Mass Society,* e.g., pp. 81–82; Elin Anderson, *We Americans* (Cambridge, Harvard Univ. Press, 1938), passim; Walker, *Steeltown,* passim; Lynd, *MIT,* passim; Jones, *Life, Liberty and Property,* passim; and esp. Peter H. Rossi, "Community Decision-making," *Administrative Science Quarterly, 1* (March 1957), 415–43.

tives presented for community decision-making seems likely, then, to be determined by considerations very different from a rational canvassing of all technically feasible possibilities. What determines the agenda of alternatives within which community decision-making takes place?

There are several plausible answers to this question, but the current state of affairs seems to be centrally important in determining the future course of action.[34] Most of the American communities studied in any detail seem to be relatively healthy political organisms, which means that there are bound to be considerable conservatism and self-preservation rather than innovation and demand for change within the system. Sayre and Kaufman suggest two reasons why this is likely to be so: in the first place:

> every modification of the existing state of affairs—of the rules, of personnel, of governmental or administrative structure or procedure, or of public policies and programs—entails the fear of cost for some participants as well as hope of gain for the proponents. . . . In most instances the costs of change are more intensely perceived by participants close to the center of decisions than are the benefits of innovation. Those who perceive the costs of change in the city's going system have strategies and weapons with which to resist. They ordinarily have prizes to withhold, inducements to offer, sanctions to impose. . . . The prospects for any advocate of change are intense opposition: lengthy, costly, wearing maneuvering and negotiation, and uncertainty about results until the last battle is won. If the anticipation of such a struggle, with all its costs in money, time, energy, and the possible disruption of longstanding friendships and alliances, is not enough to discourage campaigns in support of many proposed innovations, the strain and the drain of the *actual* fight may well exhaust the supporters and induce them to abandon their causes before they have come near their goals.
>
> In the second place, public officers and employees, whose action is required to make official the decisions reached by the participants in the specialized centers in which they operate, are ordinarily reluctant to move vigorously when there is extensive opposition within

34. Other plausible answers might be that the agenda of alternatives is determined by the ideologies of choosers; by the "real" interests of choosers; by accident; by certain underlying "structural" characteristics of the community (e.g., company town vs. dormitory suburb vs. metropolis). In presenting my own candidate for the best answer, I do not mean to exclude these possibilities. A theory that claimed some measure of comprehensiveness would probably have to consider the extent to which each of these factors determined the course of community decision-making.

the constellation of interested individuals and groups. For they, as the formal authors of changes, are most likely to bear the brunt of enmities and retaliations provoked by adverse consequences of departure from established practice. They are the visible and vulnerable targets of blame for failure, though they must often share with others any credit for achievements. Indeed, officials are understandably wary even when there is a general consensus on the desirability of a particular novelty, for they must try to take into account consequences unanticipated by the assenters. They are doubly cautious when an important and highly vocal segment of their constituency stresses the dangers and costs. So the world of officialdom is often prudent when confronted by recommendations for innovation.[35]

Dahl has suggested as a general principle that: "If A's goal requires a slight change or weak response from B, and C's goals require a great change or a strong response, then with equal resources, rates and efficiencies [of resource employment], A is more likely to succeed than C. Or, to put it another way, A can attain his political goals with *less influence* than C can. Thus, if A's goals fall well within 'political consensus' he may have to do little beyond maintaining the consensus; whereas if C's goals fall well outside the 'political consensus,' then for him to achieve his goals may require access to enormous resources."[36]

The relevance of this hypothesis to the present discussion is to suggest conditions under which the "current state of affairs," or the "political consensus" does not rather drastically restrict the array of available alternatives in community decision-making. It is not enough, as the quotations above make clear, for an alternative to be technically feasible. It also must be politically palatable and relatively easy to accomplish; otherwise great amounts of influence have to be brought to bear with great skill and efficiency in order to secure its adoption. Conclusions that might be drawn from this are that the community agenda of alternatives is relatively insensitive to any but very great differences in the power of actors and that only influence differences of the greatest magnitude as between actors are likely to be reflected in changes in the alternatives presented to decision-makers.

Community agendas, then, are hard to change. But if insensitivities to power differences distinguish the array of alternatives presented to decision-makers, similar insensitivities mark the processes of choosing among

35. Sayre and Kaufman, *Governing New York City*, pp. 716–18.
36. Dahl, "Leadership in a Fragmented Political System," p. 18.

these alternatives. The uncertainties[37] of most real-world decision-making have been well enough documented and discussed elsewhere to obviate the necessity for going into the subject once more here.[38] Only one point needs to be reiterated: many community decisions distribute many values in unintended, unanticipated ways. Finally, as I have pointed out in previous chapters, the allegedly powerful often intend, and succeed in their intention, to distribute values to the nonpowerful. All of these circumstances suggest the unwisdom of depending upon knowledge of who gets what from community decisions for the purpose of determining who rules.

WHO SUCCEEDS?

If the preceding analysis is correct, then the question "Who rules in American communities?" is in many ways devoid of meaning. Rulership, according to pluralist theory, is often characterized by (1) relatively wide sharing of powers among leaders specialized to one or a few issue-areas, calling upon many different resources and techniques for applying resources to influencing outcomes, (2) constraints upon decision-making applied by nonelites and by elites themselves, (3) conditions of all kinds imposed by impersonal outside forces, and (4) uncertainty about the distributions of payoffs of political actions. But given these conditions of modern American local life, some people attain their ends more frequently than others, and a theory of community power might reasonably be expected to explore "rulership" in this rather more limited sense of the term.

What distinguishes those who succeed from those who fail in gaining their preferences in community decision-making? Three kinds of events can be considered as, in some sense, indices of success: when an actor initiates some community policy, meets with no opposition, and it is enacted; when an actor prevents the policy of some other actor from being enacted; and when an actor initiates a policy, meets with opposition, and the policy is enacted.[39]

Success in these three situations evidently does not come automatically to possessors of great amounts of any one of the many possible resources available to actors in community life. This finding is significant not only

37. I.e., uncertainties with respect to the goals to be maximized, the best means for maximizing them, the likelihood that the best means is feasible, the possible disadvantageous by-products of various alternatives, the likelihood that these by-products will come into play if various alternatives are chosen, and so forth.
38. Robert A. Dahl and Charles E. Lindblom, *Politics, Economics and Welfare* (New York, Harper, 1953), pp. 161–68; Simon, *Administrative Behavior,* passim.
39. See Dahl, "Leadership in a Fragmented Political System."

as a statement about the real world, but for its bearing upon research strategy as well. Many resources in combination—time, knowledge, energy, esteem, money, legitimacy, and so on—must be applied with skill and diligence for actors to succeed in influencing community decisions in desired directions. This throws the focus of attention away from the sheer amount and distribution of resources available in the community to the rate and efficiency with which they are employed.

Resources and skill and diligence in exploiting them are three conditions which make for success in influencing community decisions. A fourth has been mentioned: ability to choose goals that do not strain the compliance of others in the system. A fifth condition of successful participation is closely related to the fourth: capacity to form coalitions with other participants in order to achieve one's goals. This entails choosing goals which do not preclude the possibility of joining with others; hence certain limits on the preferences of actors are implied in this condition as in the fourth. This condition for success also imposes a limitation on the strategies available to actors for achieving their goals. In order successfully to form coalitions with others, it is necessary to pursue courses of action which do not conflict with potential allies.

Certain hypotheses may be noted about coalitions.[40] They seem to come into existence in order to provide actors with the means for increasing the resources available to them in the pursuit of their own ends. We might hypothesize that *complementarity of resources* would be a powerful incentive for actors to form coalitions with one another, as, for example, an actor with popularity allying with one having wealth. A second prerequisite for the formation of coalitions would be *compatibility of goals and strategies*. Actors with different resources are not necessarily capable of pursuing compatible strategies. Furthermore, it seems likely that, given different bases of strength, their demands and expectations might diverge greatly even if their strategies were harmonized. From this hypothesis, one might deduce that the larger the coalition, the more fragile it is and the more limited its goals must be if it is to maintain itself intact and remain effective in its political environment. It seems plausible to suggest that successful coalitions are likely to be single-minded, and when coalitions take on new goals—perhaps as the result of bureaucratization—their membership may well be expected to fall away.[41]

40. Here, as elsewhere, I am drawing upon research memoranda which I wrote for the Hyde Park-Kenwood Demonstration Research Project, based on field work done in Chicago, and reported more fully in Rossi and Dentler, *Politics of Urban Renewal.*

41. The case of the Hyde Park-Kenwood Community Conference is in point. The

Perhaps the most important long-range task of a theory of community power is to distinguish among communities on the basis of their patterns of decision-making.[42] Such a theory would hopefully provide clues as to the characteristics of communities which are critically significant in determining the kinds of decision-making taking place. But before this problem can be addressed, it is necessary to reorient our expectations about the kinds of decision-making one typically finds in American communities. The literature we examined in previous chapters suggests an initial distinction between hierarchical and pluralistic decision-making patterns. However, no properly documented instances of communities where hierarchy predominates have come to light. Thus, for the moment, we are left with a plethora of independent variables, any or all of which may be sufficient conditions for the production of a single dependent variable—the pluralistic pattern of decision-making.

One might consequently expect, or hope, that the next steps in thinking about community power would be conducted along two broad lines. First, we might anticipate the differentiation of a few or several different forms of pluralistic decision-making whose course and effects could be observed in American communities.[43] Secondly, we might look forward to the identification of combinations of other features, of an economic, legal, demographic, social-structural, or cultural character, whose presence seemed to indicate the presence of one or another form of pluralistic decision-making. As studies in depth of individual communities accumulate, it will become necessary to seek devices such as this kind of comparative analysis for summarizing the information they contain. As students become increasingly concerned with satisfying the demands of scientific method and theoretical relevance in the conduct of their research, their results become more amenable to meaningful summary, and we may therefore reasonably expect the early formulation of provisional theories of community power which correspond more closely to the facts of the world around us.

Conference actually lost members over years when it was broadening its goals and increasing its staff. See Rossi and Dentler, *Politics of Urban Renewal.*

42. Harold D. Lasswell (*The Decision Process* [College Park, Md., Bureau of Governmental Research, College of Business and Public Administration, Univ. of Maryland, 1956]) gives seven categories which might be useful in developing a cross-community analysis. I have not employed them in drawing together information from a number of studies primarily because the data at hand were rather severely limited and seemed incapable of supplying sufficient information to make the introduction of this scheme worthwhile.

43. One study that makes progress in this area is Dahl's *Who Governs?*, especially in its discussion of the varieties of relationships among leaders possible in the modern American city.

Index to Authors Cited

Subject Index

"And-also" fallacy, 24, 59, 67
Atlanta, Ga., Cleaveland study of, 12 n.
 See also "Regional City"

"Bakerville," Miss., 126
Balance of power assumption, 67
Barbieri, Arthur T., 82, 83
Baton Rouge, La. *See* "Bigtown"
Bennington, Vt., 114
"Bigtown," 56–59
Boston, 12 n.
Business class: in Bigtown, 56–58; in Cibola, 59–63; in Elmtown, 31; in Middletown, 15–24; in Pacific City, 63–66; in Philadelphia, 42–44; in Regional City, 46–47, 54–55. *See also* Economic elite; Social-economic position

Case method, as substitute for theory, 122 n.–123 n.
Celentano, William, 79, 83, 84, 94, 115 n.
Chicago, 131 n.
"Cibola," 51–52, 59–63, 84, 129
Class conflict: in stratification theory, 10–11; in Bigtown, 57; in Elmtown, 32; in Middletown, 18–19, 21–23; in New Haven, 91–94; in Yankee City, 27
Cleveland, 12 n.
Coalitions, 137
"Community A," Mich., 124
Control. *See* Power
Covert power theory, 34, 51–52, 59, 67

DeVita, Henry, 84
DiCenzo, George, 83, 94

Economic dominants, in Cibola, 59–63
Economic elite: defined by Schulze, 84–85; in New Haven, 84–90; in Regional City, 46. *See also* Business class; Social-economic position
Economic leaders, in Bigtown, 56–58
"Elmtown," 30–42

"False class consciousness," 23, 67, 116; Mills on, 23 n.
Freese, Carl, 72, 87

Golden, John, 81, 82, 83, 88
Griswold, A. Whitney, 85

"Infinite regress, principle of," 34, 50–51, 59
Influence. *See* Power
Interest groups, in pluralist theory, 117
Issues, issue-areas: importance of specifying, 68, 124–28; in pluralist theory, 113–16; in Cibola, 63; in Middletown, 20; in New Haven, 69–70, 88; in Pacific City, 64–65; in Regional City, 54

"Jonesville," 7–8, 30–42

Leaders. *See* Reputational technique
Leaders, political, and ruling elite: in stratification theory, 9–10; in Elmtown, 34–36; in Jonesville, 41; in Middletown, 16–17, 19–20; in New Haven, 88–90; in Philadelphia, 43–44; in Regional City, 46, 54; in Yankee City, 28
Leadership roles, in pluralist theory, 118–19
Lee, Mayor Richard C.: called businessman by Hunter, 86 n.; and political nominations, 81–84; and public education, 77–79; and urban redevelopment, 70–76, 89
Logue, Edward, 73, 74
Lorain, Ohio, 126–27, 131 n.
"Lump of power" fallacy, 29, 67
Lynch, Frank, 83, 84, 94

Mack, Maynard, 87, 89
Metaphors, substitute for theory, 122 n.–123 n.
"Middletown," 14–24, 33 n., 107, 108 n.; leaders specialized to issue-areas, 127
Morris, Ill., 133. *See also* "Elmtown"; "Jonesville"

Yale Studies in Political Science